D0627225

A Teen
Eating Disorder
Prevention
Book

# Understanding Eating Disorder Support Groups

Heather Moehn

The Rosen Publishing Group, Inc.
New York

JERICHO PUBLIC LIBRARY

Published in 2000 by The Rosen Publishing Group, Inc.
29 East 21st Street, New York, NY 10010

Copyright © 2000 by Heather Moehn

First Edition

All rights reserved. No part of this book may be reproduced in any form without permission in writing from the publisher, except by a reviewer.

*Library of Congress Cataloging-in-Publication Data*

Moehn, Heather.
    Understanding eating disorder support groups /
Heather Moehn.
        p. cm. — (A teen eating disorder prevention book)
    Includes bibliographical references and index.
    Summary:  This book describes the most common types
of eating disorders and discusses the different forms of
support that are available for the recovery process,
including support groups, types of therapy, and more.
    ISBN 0-8239-2992-2
    1. Eating disorders—Juvenile literature 2. Eating
disorders—Treatment—Juvenile literature 3. Self-help
groups—Juvenile literature [1. Eating disorders 2. Self-help
groups] I. Title II. Series
    2000
616.85'26—dc21

*Manufactured in the United States of America*

## ABOUT THE AUTHOR

Heather Moehn is a freelance writer and editor in Boston, Massachusetts. Her nonfiction young adult books cover such diverse topics as world holidays and leukemia. She has a B.A. in English from Carleton College.

# Contents

# Part
## 1

# Understanding Eating Disorders

# 1 What Are Eating Disorders?

*At the end of finals, my friends and I go out for pizza to celebrate. I always end up stuffing myself. Then we go to an ice-cream parlor and have brownie sundaes.*
—Beth

*At track practice last week, the coach told me I would be able to run faster if I lost some weight. I've decided to go on a diet. I'm going to try to cut back on fast food and sweets, and eat more fruits and vegetables.*
—Lorrie

*When my boyfriend broke up with me, I was so depressed. I spent a week moping around the house. I ate a ton of ice cream and cookies sitting in front of the television.*
—Joanne

*After Thanksgiving dinner, I felt so full and bloated. I started to feel guilty about all*

2

*the food I had just eaten, so I went for a really long run the next day. I must have run five miles.*
—Stephanie

Do these people have eating disorders? What exactly are eating disorders? How can you tell if someone has developed one? In today's society, these are not easy questions to answer. There is so much conflicting information about what one should eat and how one should look that most people, especially teens, feel confused about food and weight. Because negative thoughts about these issues are so prevalent, it is often difficult to tell when a person has moved beyond typical diet and weight concerns and has begun to develop an eating disorder.

That is why experts place eating disorders on a broad spectrum. On one end is a normal concern for weight and appearance, while on the other end fall the extreme cases that often end in death. The American Anorexia/Bulimia Association (AABA) has created a new term, "disordered eating," to encompass the large middle area of this spectrum that includes thoughts and behaviors that are not really healthy but that are not yet so serious that they can be called eating disorders. These include dangerous or fad diets; the overuse of diet pills, laxatives, or diuretics; and abnormal eating patterns resulting in poor nutrition. The percentage of Americans with disordered eating is a staggering 80 percent. This means that only one out of five people has a healthy attitude toward food!

The girls at the beginning of this chapter probably wouldn't be diagnosed with eating disorders. Most likely those activities are isolated events that don't reflect their everyday attitudes and behaviors. But they could easily be the trigger events that lead them down the slippery slope to an eating disorder. If Stephanie's five-mile run turns into obsessive exercising to stay thin, if Joanne's one-time binge on cookies turns into a way to console herself after any troubled feelings, or if Lorrie's diet turns into severe food restrictions and results in too much weight loss, serious problems will result and professional help will be necessary to restore health.

## TYPES OF EATING DISORDERS

Although each type has unique characteristics, all eating disorders center on an obsession with food, weight, and appearance that causes health, relationships, and daily activities to suffer.

There are five main types of eating disorders. Anorexia nervosa is characterized by severe weight loss and an irrational fear of being fat. Basically, it is self-imposed starvation. People with bulimia nervosa binge on large quantities of food, then purge to remove it from their bodies, either through vomiting or the abuse of laxatives or diuretics.

Binge eating disorder, also called compulsive eating, is somewhat similar to bulimia in that people eat excessive amounts of foods, but people with binge eating disorder don't purge. As a result, compulsive eaters often become obese.

Compulsive exercising, an eating disorder that has recently become recognized as a widespread problem, involves the overuse of physical activities to burn calories. A related disorder, muscle dysmorphia, is overexercising to build up muscles and bulk.

## DIAGNOSIS OF EATING DISORDERS

Anorexia and bulimia are the only eating disorders with official diagnostic criteria. The symptoms are outlined in *The Diagnostic and Statistical Manual of Mental Disorders, Fourth Edition* (*DSM-IV*), the guide that most health professionals today use to diagnose mental disorders. People who don't have all the factors necessary for diagnosis, but who still have various traits of anorexia or bulimia, are diagnosed with Eating Disorders Not Otherwise Specified (EDNOS). This classification also includes binge eating disorder, exercise compulsion, and muscle dysmorphia. Approximately one-third of patients treated for eating disorders are diagnosed with EDNOS. Although they are not officially recognized as separate disorders, the severity of these conditions should not be underestimated.

Unfortunately, eating disorders are becoming more prevalent in today's society. The National Association of Anorexia Nervosa and Associated Disorders (ANAD) estimates that seven million females and one million males suffer from eating disorders. According to the U.S. Public Health Services Office on Women's Health, the number of sufferers today has more than doubled since the 1970s. In addition to those diagnosed with the five main disorders, a large percentage of young women's lives are affected by disordered eating attitudes and behaviors.

**Note:**
Because eating disorders affect a very large percentage of women, the feminine pronouns "she" and "her" will be used throughout the book, except in the section on muscle dysmorphia, which affects more men. This usage is not meant to downplay the seriousness of eating disorders among men. It is done simply for readability and simplicity.

## WHY DO SOME PEOPLE DEVELOP EATING DISORDERS?

Unfortunately, there is no single cause for an eating disorder, which means that there is no easy way to tell who will develop one, nor an easy way to treat it. Complicating the matter is the fact that the disorder often serves a purpose in a person's life; for instance, often it is a coping mechanism for dealing with personal problems and painful feelings. Many times, people aren't consciously aware of the deeper issues from which they are protecting themselves. As a result, even though they know their disordered behavior is dangerous, they feel that they need it in order to survive.

Despite the lack of a clear explanation for eating disorders, experts have found enough similarities between cases to point to a few factors that usually contribute. These include a complicated mix of social,

Eating disorders are often coping mechanisms that help people deal with a variety of issues, such as:

- ⊙ Painful events from the past
- ⊙ A poor sense of identity
- ⊙ Anger and negative feelings
- ⊙ Anxiety about frightening events in the future, such as growing up and leaving home
- ⊙ Loneliness
- ⊙ Lack of control in life
- ⊙ Self-hatred

psychological, and biological conditions. Thus, when a person develops an eating disorder, it may be the result of a combination of her self-image, family life, genes, and attitude toward society's ideals.

## THE ROLE OF SOCIETY: "LOOKSISM"

Our society tends to judge people based on the way they appear, and today a thin, waiflike body is considered the ideal of feminine beauty. Thus, slender people are believed to be happier and more successful, whereas overweight people are seen as unhappy and less capable. Mary Pipher, author of *Eating Pains* and *Reviving Ophelia*, describes this view as "looksism."

Girls pick up on this belief system at a very young age. While growing up, they hear many comments regarding their looks instead of their abilities. People notice how pretty a young girl is and talk about her features, such as big eyes or cute dimples. In contrast, boys usually hear remarks concerning strength, skill, and agility. Children notice the characteristics for which they receive praise and think that these characteristics are more important than other things. As a result, girls as young as preschool age consider being pretty very important; studies have shown that by the age of five, some girls are worried about getting fat.

Girls are also typically taught that they should be sweet, quiet, and agreeable, not aggressive or angry. Parents often tell girls to "act like little ladies." They are expected to place the needs of others before their own and never show negative emotions. Because young women believe they shouldn't show feelings of anger, they often turn those emotions inward. Eating disorders may result from the desire to break away from what is expected of them and the inability to express true emotions.

## THE ROLE OF THE MEDIA

The media promotes looksism by constantly showing models and actresses who are unnaturally thin. Only a handful of successful stars look like average women. A recent cover article in *People* magazine discusses the trend in Hollywood for pencil-thin actresses. "When you're an actress," says personal trainer Valerie Waters, "you're expected to maintain an ideal body weight based on an unrealistic standard."

Despite the fact that most of these women are severely restricting their calorie consumption and are probably experiencing some effects of starvation, they are seen as the height of feminine beauty. Their success, wealth, and happiness are viewed as a result of their thinness. Personal trainers worry that the need to be super skinny in Hollywood is creating some very unhealthy practices that are being emulated by the public.

Women's magazines are also a problem. Over the past few years, the models featured have become taller, thinner, and younger than in the past. The magazines contain articles that promise firmer thighs, smaller waists, and flatter stomachs with a minimal amount of work. They typically promote the idea that if women lose a few pounds, their lives will be infinitely better. This may be one reason that a vast majority of women are unhappy with their bodies. In a study by psychologist Susan Wooley, 82 percent of normal-weight women felt that they were overweight, and 45 percent of underweight women thought that they weighed too much.

- ⊙ The average American woman is 5'4" tall and weighs 140 pounds.
- ⊙ The average American model is 5'11" tall and weighs 117 pounds.
- ⊙ Most fashion models are thinner than 98 percent of American women.

Young women are particularly vulnerable to negative body image as they go through the physical changes of puberty. They admire the super thin models in teen magazines while they are gaining a little weight and developing hips and breasts. Although these are healthy, normal changes, girls are horrified that they are losing the body type that is clearly the ideal. As a result, they go to war with their bodies. In 1970, only 6 percent of teens worried about losing weight. Today that number has jumped to 40 percent. The strong desire to lose weight often results in eating disorders. In fact, approximately 86 percent of eating disorders develop before the age of twenty.

## THE ROLE OF THE FAMILY

Families provide some of the most important relationships people have throughout their lives. While growing up, people depend on their families for guidance, love, and support. Families teach morals and acceptable ways to behave. In an ideal world, all families would have good communication skills, a healthy distribution of power, the ability to solve problems, a good mix of closeness and independence, and a tolerance for change. Unfortunately, many families have difficulties with these issues. This can lead to many problems, including eating disorders.

Although every family is different, certain characteristics are often present in families with eating disorders. Maria P. Root, the author of *Bulimia: A Systems Approach to Treatment*, believes that eating disorder patients come from three types of families: the "perfect" family, the overprotective family, and the chaotic family.

## The "Perfect" Family

Members of the "perfect" family are overly concerned with how they appear to the rest of the
community. Parents in these families place a
strong emphasis on how their children look and
act and how they contribute to the family's identity. There is an implied message that appearances
are more important than what people really feel
and think. There may be many unspoken rules,
such as don't talk about our problems to anyone
outside of the family, don't do anything that would
shame the family, and always think of the family
first. Children who grow up in perfect families feel
a tremendous amount of pressure to do well and
be successful. Because it is impossible to be perfect all the time, they may find an activity at which
they can be the best—an eating disorder.

## The Overprotective Family

The overprotective family fails to establish strong
personal boundaries between members. Parents are
often involved in every aspect of their children's lives.
They have a hard time letting their children grow up,
make their own mistakes, and gain independence.
Because family members are hypersensitive to each
other, certain feelings, such as anger or sadness,
evoke very strong reactions. Often the message is
"you shouldn't feel that way," "be happy with what
you have," and "don't think of yourself all the time."

People who grow up in an overprotective family
often have a hard time with the normal separation
process that takes place during adolescence. The
responsibilities that come with choosing a college

or job, leaving home, and living on one's own are frightening to people who are overly dependent upon family members and friends to make their decisions. As a result, they may try to take control of the one area that they can—their eating habits.

## The Chaotic Family

In the chaotic family, neither parent is really available to the children. Basic rules are inconsistent or may not even exist. Children become afraid to trust, talk, or feel; as a result, they cannot deal with problems in healthy ways. Chaotic families also may have histories of abuse, alcoholism, or depression.

Singer Anne Murray's family, recently featured in a *People* magazine article about Murray daughter Dawn's fight with anorexia, would be classified as a chaotic family. Murray was often on the road when Dawn was a child. Although Dawn hated her mother leaving all the time and felt lonely, she buried those feelings because it bothered her mother to hear them. "I was trying to deal with my mom's schedule and her being away," Dawn told the reporter after treatment. "I couldn't control that, but I thought controlling my eating would help."

## THE ROLE OF BIOLOGY

Some professionals think that there may be biological and genetic factors involved in the development of eating disorders. A fact that supports this theory is that eating disorders, like many other psychiatric disorders, seem to run in families. Researchers have found that 20 percent of people suffering from anorexia have a family member with the disorder. Additionally, they found that nine out of sixteen identical twins of patients with anorexia also develop it.

When one identical twin has bulimia, there is a 23 percent chance that the other will also have it. These statistics are much higher than the rate of these disorders in the general population and strongly suggest a genetic influence.

## Hormones and Neurotransmitters

One biological factor that may be responsible is abnormalities in certain hormones and neurotransmitters. The brain controls the levels of hormones that affect appetite, body weight, mood, and responses to stress. When imbalances in these hormones are present, people may binge, purge, starve, or overexercise to compensate.

An example of this phenomenon can be seen with the neurotransmitter serotonin, which is known as "the calming chemical." A serotonin deficit has been proven to cause depression. Often people with lower levels of serotonin try to make up for it by bingeing on high-carbohydrate foods, which can lead to bulimia or compulsive overeating. At the other extreme, overly high levels of serotonin cause anxiety, obsessive-compulsive behavior, and inhibitions—all typical signs of anorexia. Restricting food intake may lower serotonin levels and make those with anorexia feel better.

## Nutrition

Certain nutritional deficiencies may also be at work. People with anorexia often have a zinc deficiency, which leads to a loss of appetite and a very delicate sense of taste. This may worsen the symptoms and lead to continuation of the disorder. However, it is not entirely clear if the nutritional problems cause the disorder or are a result of it.

## Other Possible Causes

Food sensitivities and allergies, insulin problems such as hypoglycemia, and food addictions are additional biological factors that are currently being examined. Although this way of thinking is relatively new, it shows great promise in leading to a better understanding of why some people develop eating disorders and may also lead to more effective treatments. However, some experts are very critical about this approach because it focuses solely on food, while ignoring underlying psychological problems.

## WHAT ABOUT MEN?

Although eating disorders mostly affect women, a growing number of men are diagnosed each year. It is estimated that 5 to 10 percent of eating disorder sufferers are male (this translates to about one million men). Binge eating disorder, exercise compulsion, and muscle dysmorphia are more common in men than are anorexia and bulimia. Unfortunately, because their overall numbers are so small, men with eating disorders face many more problems than women in getting diagnosed and receiving treatment.

## The Hidden Problem

Eating disorders in males are often overlooked by parents and doctors because they do not think boys are at risk. Considering that the diagnostic guidelines for anorexia in *DSM-IV* include amenorrhea (the loss of menstruation), it is clear that a gender bias exists. Although recognition of eating disorders in males is growing today, it often takes longer for men to get an accurate diagnosis. Because these disorders remain hidden for so long, they are often at a more serious stage when finally recognized.

## Gender Identity and Eating Disorders

Males often have a harder time than females admitting they have a problem with food. Because eating disorders are traditionally seen as a "women's problem," men are often afraid they will appear less of a man if they have one. This fear can be compounded if there is actual inner conflict about gender identity and sexual orientation. Studies indicate that 25 percent of eating disordered males have some homosexual tendencies. Thus, the conflicts that may lead them to develop eating disorders in the first place may also be the main reason that they do not seek help.

## Why Do Males Develop Eating Disorders?

For the most part, it seems that males develop eating disorders for many of the same reasons as women: low self-esteem, family problems, the desire to be fit, and childhood trauma. In addition, like women, men must live up to certain ideals in society. They are pressured to appear strong and in control at all times. Many feel they should not show their emotions and are afraid to seem weak.

Other reasons that males develop eating disorders are different from the reasons females do, in many respects. Men are more likely to actually have been obese before the onset of the eating disorder; the disorder often begins as a way to avoid hereditary weight-related illnesses; and they are likely to have begun dieting to enhance sports performance. Understanding the ways in which eating disorders in males both resemble and differ from those in females will undoubtedly help in diagnosis and treatment.

## Help for Males

Once an eating disorder in a male has been diagnosed, it is necessary to get help so that the recovery process can begin. Unfortunately, this is often difficult. Many residential programs are only for women, and many therapists have no experience dealing with males. Additionally, men may not feel comfortable joining a therapy group that is mostly women and focuses on issues as they relate to women. However, it has been shown that the same types of treatment work for men and women, so it is important that a man not give up hope and that he continue to search for a recovery program that is right for him.

## WHAT ABOUT ATHLETES?

Athletes, both male and female, are more at risk than the general population for developing eating disorders. Often, athletes who are already fit think that they can improve their performance by losing a few pounds. This belief may lead to drastic dieting, bingeing and purging, and excessive exercising. Ironically, instead of making them better athletes, the eating disorders make them sick, tired, weak, and unable to perform.

The extent to which eating disorders and athletics go hand in hand is evident from the results of a study conducted by Laureate Psychiatric Hospital in Tulsa, Oklahoma, with the National Collegiate Athletic Association. Researchers found that approximately 9 percent of female athletes surveyed had eating disorders severe enough to require immediate medical attention. An additional 58 percent were determined to be at high risk for developing a problem. In men, they found 10 percent with full-blown disorders; another 38 percent appeared to be at risk.

In certain sports, these numbers may actually be higher. When size and/or appearance are a factor, eating disorders are rampant. The athletes most at risk include dancers, gymnasts, figure skaters, jockeys, and long-distance runners.

## WHERE DO WE GO FROM HERE?

An eating disorder is a terrifying experience for the patient, her family, and her friends. It is important that the behavior is recognized as early as possible because the longer a person has the disorder, the harder it is to treat.

Now that we have examined some of the factors involved in the development of eating disorders, we will look in depth at the five most common disorders. Once the symptoms and signs become clear, it will be easier to tell if you or someone you know has a problem. Then we will examine the various types of professional and nonprofessional support groups that are available during the recovery process.

# 2 Anorexia Nervosa

### *Joy's Story*

*Joy, a high school senior, developed anorexia during ninth grade. That year, her parents had decided that her mother needed to go back to work as a nurse so they could start saving for college tuition.*

*Since her mother often worked late hours, Joy became responsible for her younger brother and two sisters. She was willing to help out because she felt it was her fault that her mother was working again and always tired. Every night Joy made dinner and helped her siblings with their homework. Then she decided to quit the soccer team to help out more at home. Her parents didn't ask her to, but Joy felt as if she should.*

*Without soccer practice every afternoon, Joy gained a little weight. She hated the way it felt, so she started limiting her food intake. At first she cut out only fattening and sweet things. A little of the weight came off, but Joy wanted to*

18

*lose weight faster, so she cut out all starches. It was easy because she was doing all the grocery shopping and cooking. Soon she had eliminated so many foods from her diet that she was existing on rice cakes and apples. She stopped going out with her friends on weekends because they liked pizza and Mexican food. "I have to baby-sit," she said whenever they invited her.*

*Joy still prepared elaborate dinners for her family but hardly ever ate with them. They didn't really question her claims that she had already eaten or notice that she just played with the food on her plate instead of eating it. As a result, she continued to lose weight, but it was never enough. She still felt fat. She also felt dizzy and cold all the time. One day in school, she passed out in the hallway between classes. Although the changes to her body were starting to scare her a little, Joy could not stop the dieting. The fear of getting fat was too great.*

## WHAT IS ANOREXIA NERVOSA?

The term *anorexia* comes from a Greek word meaning "loss of appetite." However, this definition is misleading. Someone with anorexia does not "lose" her appetite—in fact, she feels hungry all the time. But an irrational fear of gaining weight makes her ignore this hunger. Instead of seeing it as a healthy sign that it is time to refuel her body, a person with anorexia sees hunger as something to fight and control. She is afraid that if she begins to eat, she will lose control and not be able to stop. Every day becomes a contest between appetite and willpower. Someone with anorexia is often relieved to feel hungry because it means that there is nothing in her stomach that can make her "fat."

Being fat is the worst thing in the world to a person with anorexia, and she feels that she is fat even when she is severely underweight. No matter how many pounds are lost, it is never enough. As soon as she meets weight loss goals, new goals are set. Even when she looks skeletal, a person with anorexia will point to her thighs and stomach and claim that she needs to lose more weight.

## The Illusion of Control

This control of her appetite and weight often makes a person with anorexia feel superior to people who "give in" to their hunger. She finds a sense of power through excessive dieting and believes that it will lead to success in other areas of her life, such as popularity, grades, or athletic ability. However, even though she thinks she is strong and powerful, in reality she has lost all control. The anorexia has the real power and control in the person's life.

## HOW DOES ANOREXIA START?

People don't set out to develop anorexia. Often the behavior starts as a diet. In a society where over 40 percent of women are dieting at any given time, the fact that someone is trying to lose weight is nothing out of the ordinary. In fact, the behavior may actually be encouraged and supported. This is what happened with Maria, a seventeen-year-old who has suffered from anorexia for two years.

> *I can remember the day I started my diet. My family had just moved to a new town and school was starting in three weeks. I decided to try to lose weight before the first day of school so that I could make a good impression. My mom thought it was a great idea and began to diet with me. She bought all sorts of health foods and stopped making dessert. We weighed ourselves every day. Eventually my mom stopped. But I loved the fact that my jeans were too big. I didn't want to stop. I wanted to lose more weight. That's when it got out of control.*

When most people on diets reach their target weight, they stop trying to lose more and begin a maintenance program so that they can remain at their desired weight. In contrast, a person who is on the road to anorexia can't stop. She revels in the compliments about her new thinness and thinks that if losing a little weight feels this good, then losing more weight should be even better. Soon every aspect of her life relates to weight. She might think that if she loses ten more pounds, the cute guy in biology class will notice her, or she will be able to run faster and make it to the state track meet, or her parents will give her as much praise and attention as they give her sister.

## From Diet to Disorder

The line between dieting and anorexia is crossed when the person is no longer acting out of choice, but out of compulsion. In the clutches of anorexia, a girl's mind is consumed with thoughts of food and her actions revolve around her diet. She drops out of activities and starts avoiding social situations because she is afraid she will have to eat. Her whole personality changes. Sadly, it doesn't take long for anorexic behaviors and thinking to take over a person's life.

## WHO DEVELOPS ANOREXIA?

Experts believe that anorexia affects between 1 and 5 percent of the general population. Women make up 90 percent of sufferers. However, accurate statistics are hard to find because many people who would be diagnosed with anorexia don't think they have a problem and refuse to seek help. The typical age of onset is between thirteen and eighteen years old, but eating disorder therapists now report seeing girls who are much younger. One study of fourth grade girls indicates that 80 percent of them had already dieted.

In *The Golden Cage*, her groundbreaking book on anorexia, Hilde Bruch described the disorder as "a disease that selectively befalls the young, rich, and beautiful." At that time, it was believed that all people with anorexia were white, upper-middle class, heterosexual women. Cultural differences, experts thought, protected African-American, Hispanic, Asian, and Native American girls from developing the disorder. Now greater numbers of non-whites are seeking treatment. It is finally being acknowledged that the disease can affect anyone of any race, economic class, gender, and age.

## Common Personality Traits

It is difficult to generalize about the personalities of people with anorexia. Each person has her own history, hopes, dreams, and fears. However, psychologists have found a number of traits that are often present in young women who develop the disorder.

Peggy Claude-Pierre, founder of the Montreaux Counseling Centre for Eating Disorders in Victoria, British Columbia, coined the term Confirmed Negativity Condition (CNC) to describe the mind-set that predisposes a person to eating disorders.

CNC is characterized by a high sensitivity to the needs of others, a strong desire to please, and a strong desire to achieve. Although these are admirable qualities when possessed realistically, in someone with CNC they are expressed to such an extreme that the person stifles her own development and growth. This mind-set sends the victim the message that she is never good enough, which can lead to anorexic behavior.

## The "Model Child"

People with anorexia are often described as model children. They display perfect manners, never voice criticism, never misbehave, and rarely express anger. Their parents see them as "the ideal child" and "the one we never had any problems with." In their attempts to please everyone around them, they bury all negative feelings deep inside. But bad feelings won't stay hidden forever. In many girls they manifest themselves in the form of eating disorders.

## Perfectionism

Perfectionism is another common trait. People with anorexia are often high achievers who want to be successful and perfect. They take the ideals of society very seriously and strive to emulate their role models. They want to get the best grades, be the best athlete, and look like a fashion model.

Despite their attempts, however, people with anorexia find, not surprisingly, that they cannot live up to the unrealistically high standards that they set for themselves, and they are devastated by the smallest criticism. They are haunted by failure and always see themselves as inferior to those around them.

# WHY DO PEOPLE DEVELOP ANOREXIA?

The previous section discussed certain personality characteristics that may predispose a person to anorexia. However, not all people who show these traits develop an eating disorder. Why some people develop anorexia whereas others don't is not an easy question to answer.

It is a common misconception that people develop anorexia because they are self-absorbed, vain individuals who place too much importance on their looks and don't know when to stop dieting. This is simply not true. In reality, anorexia is a complex disorder that often begins as a way to cope with painful feelings and difficult situations that seem out of control.

People with anorexia can often point to a trigger event that set the disorder in motion. A trigger event can be something totally life changing, such as moving to a new city; leaving home for college;

being abused emotionally, physically, or sexually; or dealing with a death in the family. It can be something as simple as a comment about weight by a coach or friend.

Whatever the occurrence, it makes the person feel powerless and like a failure. Since she can't control what is happening in her life, she begins to control what she eats. This action gives her a sense of accomplishment and security.

*When I was thirteen, my parents decided to get a divorce. They told me and my sister about it at dinner one night. I remember feeling so hurt and angry that they didn't seem to care how it was going to affect us. They were just going to split and that was that.*

*Soon after, I started controlling what I ate and started eating less and less. I think that because my life was such a mess, I wanted to take charge of something. Secretly, I also hoped that being worried about me would make my parents get back together again, like they would suddenly see how much better everyone was when they were together. But really all I did was hurt myself.*

—Molly

## Family

As we saw in chapter 1, family dynamics can also be a factor in determining who develops eating disorders. A person with anorexia often comes from a family that is very concerned about appearances and always wants to seem perfect. To them, it is more important that a daughter uphold the family name than show individuality and independence. Because her identity is imposed upon her, she has no sense of her true self.

These families tend to be in the upper economic classes, and the parents provide well for their children. This can become a burden; the child feels that because her parents give her so much, she must live up to unrealistically high expectations. Many times these expectations are self-imposed. She feels she must do extraordinarily well to repay her family, so she puts tremendous pressure on herself to get all A's, win scholarships, excel at athletics, and be the best at everything she does.

Someone with anorexia is typically afraid to talk about her problems. She feels that admitting she is unhappy or in trouble would be a betrayal of her parents. Because feelings cannot be hidden forever, an eating disorder is often the way to express that there is something wrong.

*I grew up in a pretty small town and my dad was the minister of the main church. Needless to say, my family was very much in the public eye. My whole life was spent hearing about how we had a certain image to uphold and how I had to act like a minister's daughter. Every time I went out with friends I got the third degree—where are you going, with whom, when will you be back, etc.*

*When I was little, it was fine. I liked being a good girl and wearing the dresses my mom picked out for me. But as soon as I got to junior high, there were problems. I wanted to wear makeup and short skirts and hang out at the mall with my friends, but it wasn't allowed. My dad used to say, "What would the congregation think of my daughter looking like a tramp?"*

*I've had strange eating habits my whole life. When I was in second grade I would eat only grilled cheese for lunch and it had to be cut into triangles. I guess food has always been my way to express my independence. I decided to control my eating after a group of friends talked about how they all wished they were skinny. I thought, if I can't be like them and do all the fun things they're doing, at least I can be as thin as they want to be. It was also a way to revolt against my parents and do something I wanted for a change.*

—Rachel

## HOW DO YOU RECOGNIZE ANOREXIA?

Because dieting is a widely accepted—and even praised—behavior, anorexia is often not recognized until the person has suffered severe weight loss. But it is important to try to detect the disorder before it reaches such an extreme. The earlier a person gets treatment, the easier it will be for her to recover. There are often many warning signs that a person is struggling with anorexia.

### Social Withdrawal

One of the first behaviors exhibited by a person developing anorexia is withdrawal from friends and family. Often she starts to pull away even before the eating disorder begins. She may avoid family meals or gatherings and turn down invitations to social events. She is unusually afraid to eat around other people. When with a group of people, she is distracted and doesn't participate in conversations or activities. Her personality changes and she becomes sullen, tense, and depressed.

## Rituals

Another typical behavior is the use of rituals throughout the day. The purpose of the rituals may be to hide her extreme dieting from others or simply to help her get through another day without eating.

> During meals, I had a ton of bizarre activities to make it look like I was eating more than I really was. First I would cut my food into tiny pieces and spread them around the plate. When I took a bite, I'd chew it a hundred times before swallowing. If I lost count of how many times I'd chewed, I'd start all over. Often it seemed like I was chewing air. Also, after each bite, I'd take a big drink of water. That helped make me feel full. I could make a meal of about ten bites of food last as long as the rest of my family took to eat.
> —Kelly

Other common rituals include doing a form of exercise between every bite of food, not letting a utensil touch the lips, and eating the same foods every day in the same order. Rituals also can be behaviors that don't seem to have anything to do with food, like touching a certain piece of furniture when entering a room, or walking the same way to school every day. A person with anorexia becomes very strict about performing the rituals and gets upset if anyone or anything interferes.

## Obsessive Behavior

Obsessive thoughts and behaviors regarding food are another good indication that there is a problem. A person suffering from anorexia typically knows the number of calories and fat grams in every type of food and keeps track of everything that passes through her lips. She will probably limit herself to certain foods that she considers "safe," such as celery, nonfat yogurt, or apples. She insists on preparing her own food so that she knows exactly what is in it. Often, she will take control of the shopping and meal planning for the entire family.

## Physical Symptoms

There are also many physical symptoms of anorexia. A thin layer of fine, downy hair called lanugo grows all over the body. This "fur" is an attempt by the body to keep itself warm after the protective layer of fat disappears. Lanugo grows on the face, neck, hands, torso, and even in places where hair usually doesn't appear.

People with anorexia bruise easily because their body's resistance to trauma is lowered and because the bones aren't padded anymore. One woman suffering from anorexia was surprised to see big, ugly, dark bruises all over her back. They had developed from simply sitting at her desk at school because the vertebrae and the skin on her back were so unprotected.

Other changes to appearance are sunken eyes, gray or yellowed skin that often breaks out, dry

## POSSIBLE SIGNS OF ANOREXIA

⊙ Losing an excessive amount of weight within a short amount of time

⊙ Having an intense fear of gaining weight or becoming fat

⊙ Feeling that food is an enemy and that dieting has taken over her life

⊙ Thinking she is fat even though others insist she is not

⊙ Thinking in terms of "all or nothing": that food is either good or bad, that she is either thin or fat, or that she is either loved or hated

⊙ Using rituals and exhibiting strange eating habits

⊙ Missing her period for at least three consecutive menstrual cycles

⊙ Feeling cold all the time, especially in the hands and feet, which may appear blue-tinged

⊙ Rearranging schedules or stopping activities because of her preoccupation with food

⊙ Feeling depressed or anxious

⊙ Having dry, gray skin and brittle hair that falls out

⊙ Growing fine hair all over the body

⊙ Bruising easily

patchy hair that falls out in clumps, and blue-tinged fingers and toes.

## WHAT ARE THE PHYSICAL EFFECTS OF ANOREXIA?

The consequences of starvation are often deadly. It is estimated that 5 to 20 percent of people with anorexia die from complications from the disorder. One typical cause of death is cardiac failure. This is because starving leads to electrolyte imbalances that can make the heartbeat irregular.

Anorexic behavior also affects the other organs. The kidneys have a terrible strain put on them as a result of dehydration, so kidney failure is common. Because the digestive system no longer works properly, individuals suffering from anorexia usually have serious problems with their intestines and colon.

Another frightening effect of anorexia is that the organs actually shrink. In a recent study in Australia, forty-six people hospitalized for anorexia had MRI (magnetic resonance imaging) pictures taken of their brains. These were compared with control photos (photos from people without anorexia). A significant number of brains of those with the disorder showed signs of abnormalities. The brain normally has fissures, or depressions, in it. In the brains of people with anorexia, these fissures seem to be wider.

After administering various attention, memory, and visual-spatial tests, the researchers also found that the patients with anorexia did not do as well on these tasks as the control group. While it is not

certain that brain changes caused the poor performance, it is a definite possibility.

Hypoglycemia, a condition that results from low
levels of sugar in the blood, is also common. Many
people with anorexia develop osteoporosis as a result
of the loss of bone mass. As a result, their bones
become so brittle that they break easily. Insomnia,
dizziness, and depression are other possible effects.

## IS ANOREXIA WORTH FIGHTING?

Although the medical consequences of anorexia are
serious and death is a very real possibility, it is possible to recover from the disorder. People graduate
from treatment programs every day and go on to
lead normal, healthy lives. However, recovery is not
an easy process; many painful issues that have
been deeply buried must be brought out into the
open and dealt with. The disorder has been a coping mechanism for the individual, and it is usually
very difficult to let these mechanisms go.

### Act Early

It is important to get help as early as possible. The
longer a person has anorexia, the more likely she is
to die from it. For individuals who have had
anorexia for thirty years, the mortality rate is 18
percent, compared with a 5 percent mortality rate
during the first five years. However, getting help
early is often very difficult. Throughout most of the
disorder, the person with anorexia does not see her
behavior as dangerous and does not think that she
has a problem. Professional help is usually needed
to get the recovery process in motion.

# 3 Bulimia Nervosa

*I*n ninth grade I liked this guy Mike. One night I went to a football game with a group of my friends and ran into Mike and his friends there. Two other girls from our class were there and sat a few rows in front of us. They were both over-weight. Mike and this other guy started teasing them, calling them names and making fun of the way they looked. I was horrified—not because of the way Mike was treating those two girls, but because I had put on a few pounds and was afraid Mike would never like me. (It turns out I was about to grow four inches and the weight was to help my body through that.)

I immediately started a diet and the next day ate only an apple, a couple of low-fat crackers, and lots of diet soda. I kept up the diet for about a week. Then one night I was so starving that I binged. I ate everything I could get my hands on. Chips, brownies, bread with butter and peanut butter, everything. I was like a robot shoving things in my mouth.

> *Afterward I felt so sick and disgusting. I couldn't believe I had ruined an entire week of dieting. I went into the bathroom and spent a long time looking in the mirror calling myself all those names Mike had called those other girls. Suddenly it hit me: If I could make myself throw up, all that food would no longer be inside me and couldn't make me fat. I often wonder what my life would be like if I hadn't purged that night. Because life with bulimia is hell.*
>
> —Emma

## WHAT IS BULIMIA NERVOSA?

Bulimia nervosa is an eating disorder that is characterized by bingeing on large amounts of food, then purging to try to rid the body of the extra calories. The term *bulimia* comes from a Greek word meaning "insatiable appetite." It is a terrible cycle that leaves its sufferers feeling weak, guilty, ashamed, and afraid.

The binges go far beyond the overeating or splurging that happen to everyone once in a while. During a binge, a person with bulimia consumes huge quantities of food that are easily prepared and high in fat and carbohydrates, such as chips, cookies, cake, bread, ice cream, and fast food. Like Emma, people with bulimia often report feeling numb or robotic during a binge. They are able to block out any bad feelings or problems with food.

The urge to binge may come on suddenly, or the binges may be planned in advance for a specific time and place. The average binge lasts about two hours, during which over 3,000 calories are consumed. This is more than should typically be eaten in an entire day! Binges can occur once a week or, as the condition worsens, several times daily.

After a binge, people with bulimia feel an intense need to remove the food from their bodies. They might make themselves vomit, take large numbers of laxatives and diuretics, or overexercise. Purging usually brings feelings of relief and the false belief that they are back in control. However, many calories are absorbed even with purging, so in the long run this destructive practice does not lead to the expected weight loss.

## How Is Bulimia Different from Anorexia?

Bulimia is very similar to anorexia in some ways. In fact, for many years bulimia was considered to be a type of anorexic behavior, and it wasn't given a separate diagnosis until the mid-1980s. The two disorders are often called Cinderella's stepsisters. Like people with anorexia, people with bulimia have a fixation with food and weight. They have an intense fear of getting fat and see themselves as much heavier than they really are. The main difference between the two disorders is how people act out their food obsessions and fears. The person with bulimia enters the binge/purge cycle to gain control of the obsession, whereas not eating at all gives the person with anorexia a sense of power.

## HOW DOES BULIMIA DEVELOP?

Bulimic behavior often begins as a tendency to binge. Many times this is the result of a diet. Some therapists have found that people with bulimia often set themselves up for a binge by not eating regular meals. Skipping breakfast and then eating very little throughout the day leaves a person extremely hungry. At some point, the body says "enough" and by sending signals, such as intense cravings, tries to force the person to eat. It is difficult to ignore the body's messages and large amounts of food are eaten to make up for a day of starvation.

Since bingeing makes a person feel extremely uncomfortable and bloated, purging is seen as a way to eliminate the discomfort and avoid weight gain. Purging brings a great sense of relief and the feeling of control. The person no longer has to feel guilty about eating so many calories and feels drained, relaxed, and high. As the disorder progresses, she begins to purge not only after a binge but also after eating a fairly normal amount of food, anything considered "bad," and, eventually, after anything at all.

Anxiety, stress, and depression may also lead to binges. It is natural to turn to comfort foods when feeling down, but people with bulimia take this tendency too far and depend on large amounts of these foods to make them feel calm. Bingeing may also be a way to cope with painful events, such as emotional, physical, or sexual abuse, or a parent's drug problem. The numbness and relief experienced during a binge replace all other thoughts, actions, and emotions. However, the feelings of serenity and comfort are very short-lived. They are soon replaced by guilt and fear. So the person with bulimia purges to try to lessen the shame of the binge.

## The Illusion of Control

In the beginning, most people believe that they are in control of this behavior and that they can stop at any time. In a way, bulimia increases their confidence—they think they have found a way to lose weight while still eating all they want. However, it doesn't take long before food becomes the dominant force in their lives. Instead of going out with friends and being involved in activities, people with bulimia are constantly planning the next binge and thinking of where they can get food. They are ashamed of this behavior and are afraid of being "found out," so they retreat from their friends and become very secretive. Before they know it, the binge/purge cycle has taken over their lives.

## WHO DEVELOPS BULIMIA?

Bulimia is very widespread and much more common than anorexia. Experts estimate that 8 to 10 percent of adolescent and college women suffer from bulimia. Other studies show that as many as 25 to 30 percent of college-age women practice binge/purge behaviors for weight control. Of all people with bulimia, 10 percent are men.

The typical age of onset is sixteen to eighteen years old. This is the age where young adults gain more personal freedom, have their own money, and are able to spend more time away from their families. Thus they have the time, privacy, and income to allow for binges and purges. Bulimia is sometimes thought to be a learned behavior. It is rampant at boarding schools and on college campuses where girls often share "tips" on staying thin while eating whatever they want. In many lavatories in girls' dorm buildings, students complain that they often smell vomit and that the pipes are frequently clogged.

## Personality and Bulimia

Although bulimia and anorexia are closely linked, there are significant personality differences in people with the disorders. People with bulimia tend to be less self-controlled and more impulsive than people with anorexia. They often show obsessive-compulsive tendencies and are more likely to abuse drugs and alcohol and engage in unhealthy sexual relationships.

Like people with anorexia, most people with bulimia tend to be uncomfortable with close, intimate relationships. The bulimia becomes their best friend, and they believe that it is the only thing they can count on.

Many people who develop bulimia were also considered ideal children. They are people-pleasers who put more emphasis on how others see them than on how they actually feel. Because they want to be perfect, they are overly judgmental of themselves, fear criticism, and avoid disagreements. They have low self-esteem and feel insecure about their appearance, abilities, and value. Bingeing helps relieve their feelings of inadequacy and gives them a temporary feeling of control.

## WHY DO PEOPLE DEVELOP BULIMIA?

Many of the reasons people develop bulimia are very similar to the reasons people get anorexia. Among these are low self-esteem, childhood conflicts, a feeling of helplessness, and a fear of becoming fat. As with anorexia, bulimia often begins during a life transition that leaves a person feeling out of control, such as moving, leaving home, or ending or beginning a significant relationship. Instead of finding control in restricting food intake like people with anorexia, individuals with bulimia binge to calm the negative feelings, then purge to regain a feeling of control.

## The Role of the Brain

If the underlying reasons are so similar, why do some people develop bulimia, whereas others develop anorexia? The answer to that question may be biological. Scientists have recently begun to understand how chemicals and neurotransmitters in the brain affect mood and appetite. An imbalance in these chemicals may affect how a person approaches food.

When certain neurotransmitters, such as serotonin and norepinephrine, do not function properly, a person may become depressed. Depression is very common in people with bulimia. In fact, it is so prevalent that some experts think bulimia may be a form of depression instead of a separate eating disorder. Many times, when the depression is treated with drugs, the bulimic behaviors disappear.

Scientists have also found biochemical similarities between people with bulimia and those with obsessive-compulsive disorder (OCD). This anxiety disorder is characterized by uncontrolled, continuous, abnormal thoughts (such as violence, fear of contamination, or worrying about a tragic event) and compulsive actions taken in response to the obsession. The behaviors often are seemingly senseless, ritualistic, and repetitive. An example of an obsessive-compulsive person is someone who is obsessed by thoughts of uncleanliness and spends several hours a day washing and rewashing his or her hands. Some aspects of bulimia are very similar to obsessive-compulsive behavior. Just as the action of handwashing relieves the tension surrounding thoughts of uncleanliness, bingeing and purging reduces the anxiety surrounding food. Studies are currently being conducted to determine if bulimia is a variation of obsessive-compulsive disorder.

## The Role of the Family

Family dynamics also play a role in the development of bulimia. According to *Bulimia: A Guide for Recovery,* 91 percent of people with bulimia surveyed felt that their families had contributed to their disorder in some way. Many individuals with bulimia come from dysfunctional families where they may not have received the support that they needed or learned how to handle stress.

Often the parents are too busy or preoccupied with their own problems to pay enough attention to the children. Thus a person with bulimia grows up thinking she is not worthy of her parents' time and has to rely on herself. She blames herself and thinks there must be something wrong with her. She fears rejection and does not want to seem too needy, so she buries these feelings.

Also, many people who develop bulimia have grown up in families with a history of drug abuse, depression, or eating disorders. While such a history may genetically predispose someone to substance abuse, having these problems in the family also teaches a child to turn to exterior sources for mood control. Instead of looking within themselves for the source of conflicts, people with bulimia turn to food, and often to drugs and alcohol.

## HOW DO YOU RECOGNIZE BULIMIA?

Bulimia can be very difficult to detect. Unlike anorexia, which leaves its sufferers looking skeletal and sickly, people with bulimia are usually of average weight and look fairly normal. Complicating the matter is the fact that they are very secretive about their eating behaviors. People with bulimia usually don't binge in front of other people and will purge only in privacy. While fighting the disorder, many people with bulimia are able to lead very successful lives. Nevertheless, there are both psychological and physical warning signs that can be spotted.

### Behavioral Warning Signs

Unusual or varying eating habits are one clue. Many people with bulimia do not like to eat in public and will often try to avoid it. If it can't be avoided, a person with bulimia will often carefully watch what she eats. She will stick to healthy, low-fat choices and eat very little. This hides both her fear of food and her fear that she will lose control.

Once in private, however, she will consume large quantities of the foods she deprived herself of during the day. At other times, if she knows she will be able to purge afterward, a person with bulimia will eat much more than usual and eat things she typically would avoid.

People with bulimia often develop strange ideas about how food affects their bodies. After eating, someone with bulimia may become very agitated as a result of these irrational thoughts. She will probably want to purge and may head straight for the restroom. If she cannot get the necessary privacy and is unable to purge, she may become very upset and feel that the food is instantly turning into fat. People with bulimia have a constant fear of becoming fat, even though they are usually within a normal weight range. They are also preoccupied with their appearance. They may weigh themselves several times a day and often look in mirrors to see how their clothes fit.

As the disorder develops, a person with bulimia will spend more and more time alone. She will avoid social situations, especially ones where food is involved. In contrast to the majority of people with anorexia, most people with bulimia realize that what they are doing is unhealthy and are ashamed of the fact that they can't stop, so they withdraw from friends and family and refuse to talk about what is bothering them.

Many people with bulimia hide food to eat in later binges. Often finding this food or evidence of a binge is a key to recognizing bulimia.

*My best friend was recently diagnosed with bulimia. It turns out she has been this way for years and years without anyone knowing. Losing weight was very important to her. She constantly commented on how fat she was and how she needed to lose ten pounds. During the day she would either skip lunch or eat salads with no dressing. It seemed like she was so in control of her eating that I couldn't understand why she didn't lose weight.*

*One day when her parents were out of town, we planned to study at her house. I went over about a half hour early and found her in the kitchen. There was food every-where—cookie boxes, chips, crackers, even cake batter. It looked like there had just been a party. I had no idea what to think. Then, when she saw me, she burst into tears and ran into the bathroom. I could hear her getting sick. Suddenly I realized what was going on. I told her she had to tell someone or I would. When her parents came home, she told her mother and is now seeing a psychologist a few times a week.*

*—Michaela*

## Physical Warning Signs

Besides these behavior patterns, there are many physical signs of bulimia. Constant vomiting causes salivary glands to become infected and swollen, making the person's face unusually puffy and round. The enamel on her teeth erodes, causing decay and often bad breath. Her eyes may be red as a result of broken blood vessels, and her skin will become dry and pasty.

Another clue is bruised or callused knuckles and scratches or bite marks on her fingers from induc-ing vomiting. Hands and feet are usually cold and tingly because of poor circulation caused by low potassium levels and other vitamin deficiencies.

## POSSIBLE SIGNS OF BULIMIA

⊙ Experiencing recurring episodes of binge eating followed by purging activities

⊙ Feeling out of control during a binge

⊙ Basing self-worth on weight and body shape

⊙ Feeling that food is taking over her life

⊙ Fearing the loss of control around food

⊙ Having an intense fear of gaining weight

⊙ Planning and preparing for binges ahead of time

⊙ Going to the restroom soon after eating in order to purge

⊙ Suffering from swollen glands, sore throat, dizziness, and cramps caused by binge/purge behavior

⊙ Having bruises, scrapes, and scars on fingers from inducing vomiting

## WHAT ARE THE EFFECTS OF BULIMIA?

The physical effects of bulimia are very serious. The longer a person continues this behavior, the more severe the symptoms will become and the longer it will take for her body to recover.

Because of the constant loss of fluid through vomiting or use of laxatives or diuretics, the chemicals in the body of someone with bulimia are unbalanced. These chemicals, such as potassium, are very important in regulating bodily functions. With low levels of potassium, a person with bulimia may suffer from muscle weakness and heart arrhythmia (an irregular heartbeat). When the imbalance of electrolytes becomes great enough, death by cardiac arrest sometimes occurs.

Most people with bulimia also experience problems with their intestines and bowels. Laxative abuse can damage nerve endings in the intestines and make the bowels lose muscle tone, which can inhibit these muscles from contracting. As a result, constipation or diarrhea is a common occurrence. People who abuse laxatives also frequently develop rectal pain, gas, and bowel tumors.

People with bulimia often complain about sore throats. Repeated vomiting irritates the esophagus, the passage from the stomach to the mouth. They may develop blisters or ulcers in the esophagus. In extreme cases, the esophagus or stomach may even rupture.

The acid from vomit will decay tooth enamel, so most people with bulimia have very bad teeth. In fact, it is sometimes the dentist who will be the first to notice symptoms of bulimia during a dental exam. The erosion results in irritation of the mucous membranes, dryness in the mouth, scaling on the surface of the lips and mouth, and sensitivity to hot and cold. Other side effects of bulimia include severe dehydration, digestive disorders, malnutrition, amenorrhea, infected glands, internal bleeding, anemia, and hypoglycemia.

## IS BULIMIA WORTH FIGHTING?

As is true of anorexia, bulimia is definitely worth fighting. In fact, if the recovery process is not begun, the behavior could end in death. Some professionals feel that recovery from bulimia is easier than recovery from anorexia because people with bulimia usually recognize that their behavior is dangerous and are often more willing to accept help. However, because the binge/purge behavior has been protecting the sufferer from dealing with painful issues, it can be extremely difficult to give up this behavior.

Because bulimia wasn't recognized as a separate disorder until about a decade ago, long-term recovery statistics are not available. A recent study indicated that three years after treatment, 27 percent of people with bulimia binge and purge less than once a month; 33 percent still binge and purge almost daily; and the remaining 40 percent fall somewhere between the two.

# 4

# Binge Eating Disorder

*During math class, the teacher asked Cassandra to go up to the board to work out a problem. While she was standing at the front of the class, she could hear people whispering and giggling behind her back. She was so conscious of everyone looking at her that she couldn't concentrate on the problem. She should have known the answer, but she couldn't think clearly. She could feel her face turning red and tears pricking her eyes.*

*Finally the teacher said she could go back to her seat and called someone else to work out the problem. Humiliated, Cassandra sat down. "Thank god lunch is next period," she thought as she walked back to her desk. Right after class, she went to the McDonald's drive-through and ordered enough food for three people. She sat in the parking lot and ate it all.*

## WHAT IS BINGE EATING DISORDER?

Binge eating disorder (BED) is the most recently recognized category of eating disorders. The term was officially introduced in 1992 at an International Eating Disorders Conference. Binge eating disorder (sometimes referred to as compulsive overeating, emotional overeating, and food addiction) is characterized by consuming excessive amounts of food within a relatively short period of time. In this sense, it is similar to bulimia. The main difference is that binge eaters do not purge after eating.

Some experts make a distinction between binge eating disorder and compulsive overeating. Many binge eaters eat normally during the day when other people are around, then binge in private. In contrast, compulsive overeaters may "graze" all day. In addition to three main meals, they also have many smaller meals and snacks. Jill and Colleen's behavior are examples of the two different disorders.

*For years I felt like I was leading a double life. During the day, I would seem like a normal person. I would eat a bowl of cereal with my brother in the morning, then a salad or sandwich for lunch at school. But as soon as school was over, I would lose control. The grocery store was on my way home, so I would stop and get tons of food. I'd eat most of it in the car on the way home, then finish the rest up in my room while I was "studying."*
—Jill

*I was always a chubby kid, which led to lots of teasing from people at school. I never had really good friends and I felt very lonely growing up. Food was the only thing I felt I could count on to always be there for me. And it was—I ate all day long. The first thing I thought of when I woke up in the morning was breakfast. Then all morning I dreamed of lunch. As soon as lunch was over, I was thinking about dinner. And in between those big meals, I snacked. People joked that they never saw me without some kind of food in my hands. It was my shield.*
—Colleen

As a result of overeating without compensatory behavior, many people with the disorder become obese. The definition of obesity is that a person's body weight is approximately 25 percent more than what is considered a normal range for his or her height and build. Experts estimate that approximately one-third of obese patients seeking treatment engage in binge eating. However, not all people who are binge eaters become overweight. It is entirely possible to be a compulsive eater and remain at a normal weight range.

No matter what their method of overeating, compulsive and binge eaters all have a few things in common. They no longer recognize their bodies' signals indicating when they are hungry or full, and they eat regardless of whether or not they are actually hungry. Their thoughts are usually consumed by food. Compulsive eaters also continually feel out of control. In addition, most deal with the stigma of being overweight in a society that idealizes thinness. Many people think that they just need "a little willpower" to lose weight. As you are learning, however, the issues are much deeper than that.

## HOW DOES BINGE EATING DISORDER DEVELOP?

### Excessive Dieting

As with other eating disorders, binge eating often begins as a diet. Most diets require people to avoid certain foods, go for long periods of time without eating, and eat very small portions. Dieting is not a healthy way to live. Following such strict rules usually results in strong cravings. Even dieters with the best intentions find it hard to follow a diet for a long period of time. After a while, they feel they must give into their cravings. This often results in binge eating.

### Learned Habits

Compulsive eating may also develop from habits learned as a child. Many families have rules such as "You must finish everything on your plate." This teaches children to eat until all the food is gone, even if they are no longer hungry. As a result, they lose the ability to tell if they are full or not. As long as there is still food in front of them, they eat.

### Food and Feelings

Many families also use food as a reward or punishment. People often celebrate special events by going out for ice cream or making a special dessert. Similarly, they may send children to their rooms without dinner or take away dessert as a punishment. This type of behavior places an emotional emphasis on food. Instead of thinking of food as simply fuel that your body needs, people begin to see food as a way to comfort and reward themselves.

## WHO DEVELOPS BINGE EATING DISORDER?

Compulsive eating and BED are the most common eating disorders. BED is found in about 2 percent of the general population (one to two million people). However, experts have estimated that as many as sixty to seventy million people suffer from some form of compulsive eating. In *Overcoming Binge Eating*, Dr. Christopher Fairburn reports that one in every five young women engages in binge eating.

Of all the eating disorders, BED affects the most diverse group of people. It is found in people of all ages, economic classes, and cultures. It affects just as many blacks as whites. More men suffer from BED than any other eating disorder, although the majority (85 percent) of compulsive eaters are women.

Often BED is a learned behavior within families. When parents control their emotions with food, children start to do the same. Lorraine believes her mother contributed to her binge eating disorder.

*When I was little, my mom rarely ate dinner with us because she was always dieting. Instead, she would eat all the leftovers when we were done (and there were usually a ton). She would also eat entire tubs of ice cream or bags of cookies whenever something stressful happened. I think I got a lot of my habits with food from observing her. I always turn to junk food when I feel bad, and though I never let other people see me pig out, I binge in private at least twice a week.*

## WHY DO SOME PEOPLE BECOME COMPULSIVE OVEREATERS?

There are two main theories about why some people become compulsive overeaters. One points to biological factors, whereas the other sees psychological factors as the main reason. It seems that most people with compulsive overeating develop the disorder as a result of a combination of these two factors.

### Biological Factors

Doctors who believe biology plays a large role point to chemical imbalances in the brain as a reason some people compulsively overeat. Serotonin is one of the main chemicals linked to mood and appetite. Recent studies have found that a normal amount of serotonin reduces depression, helps people sleep, and tells their brains when they are full after a meal. If someone has a low level of serotonin, he or she may try to create its effects artificially. This can result in binge eating.

People with food sensitivities or allergies are also more at risk for developing binge eating disorder. When someone has a food sensitivity, his or her body cannot completely digest the food's proteins. The proteins are then seen as foreign substances.

The body produces antibodies to fight the undigested proteins each time the person eats that food. Ironically, this is thought to cause intense cravings for the very food that is causing the reaction. Allergies to sugar and white flour are common. Hence, these foods are often eaten in large quantities during a binge.

A condition called hypoglycemia may also cause binge eating patterns. It is often described as the opposite of diabetes. Instead of producing too little insulin, hypoglycemics have too much. As a result, their blood sugar is processed too quickly, which makes it suddenly fall to low levels. This can have the drastic side effects of intense hunger, confusion, inability to concentrate, anxiety, and depression.

Sugar gives a quick burst of glucose to the system, so hypoglycemics often turn to sweet foods to relieve low blood sugar. However, this relief is short-lived as the pancreas produces insulin and the sugar is quickly processed. Unfortunately, this eating pattern produces a yo-yo effect: Sugar is ingested to produce a quick high; the sugar is quickly processed, producing a crash; then more sugar is needed to keep the symptoms of low blood sugar away.

## Psychological Factors

Most therapists feel that psychological factors almost always play a role in compulsive overeating. They feel that it is important to distinguish between the two types of hunger people experience. Physical hunger is what you feel around mealtimes when your stomach growls and feels uncomfortable. People who feel emotional hunger eat to fill an emptiness caused by sadness or depression. Compulsive eaters often eat for emotional reasons instead of physical ones. Food is used as a coping mechanism. By focusing on bingeing, they can avoid confronting painful and difficult issues in their lives.

Loneliness is a common reason compulsive eaters give for their behavior. This was definitely the case with Brenda, a high school senior.

*The summer before sophomore year in high school, my dad got transferred to a new city. I really didn't want to move. I had a ton of good friends at my old school and was really into theater. I love acting and being up on stage in front of an audience. My new school is really small and doesn't even have a drama department. Since the kids have known each other since kindergarten, they are really cliquey and don't even bother to get to know new people. Junior year was awful. No one would sit with me in the cafeteria, so I started going out for lunch.*

*I found that food numbed my sad feelings, so I would go to three or four different fast food places and eat complete lunches at each one. I gained a lot of weight, which made me feel even worse about myself. This year, my senior year, I'm getting it under control. I've joined a support group and am focusing on getting into a good college where I can start over and make some great new friends.*

Many people, especially women, binge eat to cover feelings of anger. Society places women in the role of caregivers. From a young age they are taught to put the feelings of others first and not to express any negative feelings. As a result, many women suppress their feelings and are unable to resolve conflict in a healthy way. Binge eating is often a way to numb the frustration this can lead to.

Compulsive eating can also be a way to cope with family dysfunction or abuse. Compulsive overeaters who are victims of abuse use the disorder to block out their negative feelings. It can also be a protective device, especially with those who have suffered sexual abuse. Girls who have been sexually abused may overeat and gain weight as a way to appear less attractive in terms of society's ideals. They think that if they look unattractive, the abuse will stop. Eating is also something they can control when the rest of their world seems completely out of their control.

*My dad is an alcoholic. The worst is when he comes home drunk. He starts slamming doors, hitting walls, and shouting. Sometimes he hits my mom or me. I know to get out of the way when he acts like that. I go up to my room and turn on my stereo really loud. I have a stash of food under my bed for these times. I eat candy bars, cupcakes, and potato chips until I have completely blocked out everything. Afterward, I feel so sick that I can only lie down and cry myself to sleep.*
—Maura

Growing up can be a scary thing. It is a time of change, both emotional and physical. Young adults are expected to take on more responsibility and make their own decisions. For some, like Denise, this causes a great deal of anxiety. Overeating can be a way of calming fear and avoiding stressful things.

*I really liked high school and had good friends. Halfway through my senior year, I realized it wasn't going to last forever. My friends were all applying to different colleges, some really far away. I had no idea what I wanted to do and became almost paralyzed whenever I thought about it. At the same time, my parents started getting really concerned about my future. They would start out having "discussions" with me about it that always turned into shouting matches. I felt stressed out all the time.*

*One day, I was up in my room trying to fill out a college application. I had a bag of cookies and suddenly realized that I had eaten the entire bag. Strangely enough, I felt much better and much less anxious. So now I eat bags of cookies and other things any time I feel stress (which is almost all the time). I know it isn't normal, but I can't seem to stop.*

Because emotional factors usually play a big role in compulsive overeating, dieting to lose weight will not work. Before a compulsive overeater can tackle the issue of weight, the person needs to figure out the emotional reasons he or she overeats. This can be extremely difficult. The behavior has made it possible to hide from and avoid thinking about the deeper issues. Therefore, professional help, such as therapy, is usually necessary.

## HOW DO YOU RECOGNIZE BINGE EATING DISORDER?

It is often hard to tell who is a binge eater. Since BED is not officially recognized as an eating disorder, there are no definite diagnostic criteria. However, the *DSM-IV* lists certain behaviors to help professionals recognize the condition.

One such behavior is that the binge eating occurs, on average, at least two days a week for at least six months. The binges are characterized by eating a significantly larger amount of food than a normal person would consume in the same time period. During this time, there is the sense that the person cannot control his or her actions and is unable to stop.

According to the *DSM-IV* guidelines, at least three of the following behaviors are present during a binge: eating faster than normal, eating until feeling extremely full, eating even when not feeling hungry, eating alone because of shame, and feeling disgusted and depressed after overeating.

Because binges usually occur in private, it is difficult for most people to use these guidelines to determine if a loved one has a problem. However, there are a few behaviors that can be watched for that indicate binge eating disorder.

### Unhealthy Dieting

Many binge eaters have a history of yo-yo dieting. They will try anything to get their eating habits under control and always hope that the latest fad diet will be the answer. A new diet may result in some weight loss, but soon they find they cannot maintain it and the pounds come back. As a result, they are often on a roller coaster ride of weight gain and weight loss.

Some claim to keep to a strict diet and do not eat anything "bad" around other people. If they do not lose any weight despite this rigid control in public, it is a likely sign of secret binges. Others may be more open about their eating habits. You will see them eating at all times of the day and eating more than seems necessary.

## An Expensive Habit

Binge eating is very expensive. Large grocery bills are clear indications. But the more subtle disappearance of money without any new purchases can also be a clue. This is how Tanya's parents discovered her binge eating disorder.

*I worked at a trendy clothing store after school and on weekends. The money was supposed to go into my savings to help pay for college. But every time I got paid I went on a binge. I really didn't like the job and I was scared about going to college, so I guess I was trying to sabotage both those things.*

*Before I knew it, all the money was spent on pizza, candy, and junk food. My dad finally checked my bank account and realized there was no money there and confronted me. I was so embarrassed. But I knew I had a problem and wanted to get help, so I told him everything.*

*Now I am going to a support group that is helping me cope with all my feelings instead of burying them with food.*

## Hiding Food

Hidden food is also a sign. Many binge eaters stash food in their closets, under beds, in cars, and in lockers. They often carry candy bars or other snacks with them during the day. This gives them a

### POSSIBLE SIGNS OF BINGE EATING DISORDER

⊙ Eating throughout the day, even when not hungry

⊙ Bingeing for no apparent reason

⊙ Feeling guilty and remorseful after overeating

⊙ Planning secret binges ahead of time

⊙ Spending a lot of money on food

⊙ Thinking about food a great deal of the time

⊙ Eating sensibly in front of others, then bingeing in private

⊙ Feeling unhappy because of eating habits

⊙ Eating when stressed or upset

⊙ Allowing eating habits to affect all aspects of life

sense of comfort. They know if anything bad happens, food is there to numb the feelings.

## WHAT ARE THE EFFECTS OF BINGE EATING DISORDER?

Binge eating takes a heavy emotional and physical toll on its sufferers. Emotionally, compulsive overeaters have a poor self-image and constantly feel guilty and ashamed about their behavior. As a result, they crave approval from others, yet are unable to form intimate relationships. They find it difficult to talk openly about their emotions and often feel powerless and depressed.

The emotional effects of binge eating are part of a vicious circle. A compulsive overeater eats because she has a poor self-image. The binges make her feel guilty and ashamed, which creates more damage to her fragile self-esteem and thus causes her to binge again.

The physical dangers of BED are often a result of obesity. In many people, being overweight causes high cholesterol, which can lead to clogged arteries and heart attacks. The likelihood of high blood pressure is also increased, which can result in heart disease and kidney, liver, and lung damage. There is also a higher incidence of strokes, which are caused by blocked blood vessels in the brain.

Obese people are also at higher risk for certain forms of cancer. Many obese people also get diabetes, which can lead to blindness, poor circulation, and death. Obesity is also linked to fertility problems. When an obese person is pregnant, it is considered high risk and the pregnancy will have to be carefully monitored.

In addition, BED often leads to other forms of eating disorders. If a binge eater is afraid of gaining too much weight, she may begin to purge after bingeing (bulimia) or not eat at all (anorexia).

## IS BINGE EATING DISORDER WORTH FIGHTING?

Although the direct side effects of binge eating disorder are not as serious as those of anorexia and bulimia, it often leads to obesity, which can create major health problems. The psychological damage from the disorder is also very serious and greatly affects the way that people live their lives. For these reasons, it is definitely worth fighting BED.

It is important for people to remember that this is a very common disorder. There are many support groups and therapists in every community to help. Dieting alone is not the answer. Gaining control of this problem requires a change in the way a person views her life. New behaviors and new ways of thinking are necessary, and it often takes professional help to gain that insight.

# Compulsive Exercise Disorder and Muscle Dysmorphia

*A*ngie pushed the button, making the tread-mill speed up. She had already been on it for forty-five minutes, but she wasn't anywhere close to being done exercising. Today was her best friend Lydia's birthday and her friends had brought chocolate cake to eat after lunch. At first Angie had said she didn't want any, but everyone made such a big deal about it. "You're so skinny," her friends said. "You don't have to worry about a piece of cake." Besides, it looked so good and rich. Her mouth had started water-ing just thinking about it. So she had eaten a big piece with ice cream, too.

Now Angie was angry with herself. "A week's worth of dieting down the tube," she thought. After an hour and a half on the tread-mill, she rode the exercise bike for a half hour until a step aerobics class started. As she left the gym, she felt so lightheaded that she was afraid she would pass out. But at least she didn't feel so guilty about the cake anymore.

# WHAT IS COMPULSIVE EXERCISING?

Compulsive exercising is also known as exercise bulimia or exercise addiction. It is similar to bulimia in that a person purges calories from her system. However, a compulsive exerciser, instead of vomiting or abusing laxatives, exercises an extreme amount. Compulsive exercising is closely linked with other eating disorders, such as bingeing, restricting food, and purging through vomiting or laxative abuse, and compulsive exercisers often show symptoms of these other disorders.

## What Is Muscle Dysmorphia?

A related disorder is muscle dysmorphia. Instead of viewing themselves as too fat and big, people with this disorder see themselves as too small and weak. They spend countless hours at the gym trying to gain muscle and increase their size.

*I wanted to play football in high school. I had played in junior high and was pretty good, so I assumed I had a good chance of making the team. But when I showed up for tryouts, I couldn't believe how big all the other guys were. I hadn't changed much from eighth to ninth grade, but most of the other guys had grown a ton and filled out. Not surprisingly, I got creamed during the practices that week and didn't make the cut.*

*I decided that I was going to come back the next year and wow them all. I immediately began taking supplements and drinking protein shakes. I also spent every morning before school and every afternoon after school at the gym. I lifted weights like crazy. The thought of getting bigger totally consumed me. I hardly made any new friends that year and missed a lot of fun events like homecoming and other dances because I couldn't take the time to ask someone to go with me. My life was on hold until I met my goal of being a muscular jock.*

*Finally, a year went by and it was time for football tryouts again. I made the team, but I was so burnt out and fed up that I wasn't even excited. I realized how insane I had become and decided to cut back on the weights and workouts and just do my best at practices. I never became a standout, but my life became more balanced.*

—Peter

## HOW DOES COMPULSIVE EXERCISING DEVELOP?

In recent decades, people have become more aware of the connection between exercise and health. Moderate exercise lowers blood pressure and reduces the risk of many illnesses. Unfortunately, many people do not exercise for the health benefits—they care only about the physical effects. They want to lose weight, get a flat stomach, or increase muscle mass. When this is the mind-set during exercise, it can easily turn into a compulsion.

Compulsive exercising usually begins with the desire to be thin. Someone who develops this disorder may begin a diet by restricting calories. If they slip while on the diet (as most people do), they turn to exercise to compensate for the "extra" food they have eaten. Alternately, they may have begun an exercise program to lose a little weight. When it works, they think, "If I can lose that much weight by working out thirty minutes a day, imagine what I could lose if I exercised for an hour or two."

Muscle dysmorphia, on the other hand, begins with the desire to bulk up. It may be triggered by a comment from a coach or a friend, or a feeling of inadequacy. As it develops, the need to lift more weight and get bigger becomes more important than anything else in life.

> *I work out at least three hours every single day. I get up early to go for a long run before school; then after school, I go to my gym and take two aerobics classes. During school I am always fidgeting and doing little muscle flexes at my desk. My friends all say that I am so good and that they wish they had my discipline. It drives me crazy. Can't they see that I'm miserable? I hate the way I am. I want to be able to stop, but I can't. I feel like if I miss one workout, I'll turn into a big tub of fat.*
> —Julia

## WHO DEVELOPS AN EXERCISE ADDICTION?

The profile of a compulsive exerciser is very similar to that of someone with anorexia or bulimia. Compulsive eaters are usually perfectionists, very sensitive, intelligent, and intensely driven. The disorder most often affects people in their late teens and twenties. Although there are no exact statistics describing how much of the population this disorder affects, some experts believe that out of the 30 percent of Americans who say they exercise regularly, at least a third are addicted to exercise. The American Anorexia/Bulimia Association estimates that about 50 percent of women with anorexia and bulimia also overexercise to lose weight.

More men than women develop muscle dysmorphia. This may be because in today's society the ideal male has broad shoulders, big biceps, and a narrow waist. Although men are not held to as strict a standard as women, male actors and models strive to achieve this ideal body type.

## WHY DO PEOPLE BECOME ADDICTED TO EXERCISE?

The reasons people develop an addiction to exercise are very similar to the reasons people develop the other eating disorders we have examined. In fact, compulsive exercising is often a part of one of the other disorders. There are a variety of social, biological, and medical reasons that people may turn to exercise addiction.

### Thin Is In

The desire to obtain what is considered the ideal body is a commonly stated cause of this disorder. Compulsive exercisers think that if they work out long and hard enough, they will look like models and actors. They equate happiness and success with being thin and fit. Adding to the problem is the fact that compulsive exercisers are usually encouraged in their pursuit of fitness. Sufferers are commended for their discipline, and others envy their stamina. They enjoy the attention and praise that staying fit brings them and this encourages them to exercise even more. Unfortunately for people with exercise addiction, exercise is viewed as a positive activity and people rarely see the dangers.

People with muscle dysmorphia have a very similar mind-set and are just as preoccupied with their bodies as people with other disorders. Most feel that their success depends upon how they look. Often males with the disorder believe that if they were more muscularly built, girls would want to date them, they would be more successful in sports, and they would become more popular. Unfortunately, the disorder usually has the opposite effect, causing sufferers to limit activities and end friendships to allow for more exercise time.

## Exercise as a Coping Mechanism

Compulsive exercising can also be used as a coping mechanism. If there are painful and difficult issues occurring in his or her life, a compulsive exerciser can forget all about them during a ten-mile run, an hour on the stepper machine, or an evening spent lifting weights. Exercising can be a way to block out negative thoughts and feelings.

## HOW DO YOU RECOGNIZE COMPULSIVE EXERCISING?

In all of the disorders discussed in this book, it is often difficult to tell when a person moves from a healthy attitude to a compulsion. For compulsive exercisers, the main clue is when exercise takes over the person's life. Compulsive exercisers don't let anything get in the way of their workout. They usually have a strict schedule and will rearrange their activities around a certain aerobics class or a daily run. They may even go so far as to drop out of events and stop hanging out with friends and family.

> *It took a long time for me to realize that my exercising was getting out of control. It finally hit me one day as I was arguing with my mother about going to my grandfather's nine-tieth birthday celebration. The party was on a Sunday afternoon and I had planned on running a half-marathon that day. It wasn't a real road race that I had entered. I was just going to go on my own. My mother got furious that I was going to choose running over seeing my grandfather. His health wasn't that great and he wasn't expected to live much longer. "Just think about how you'll feel if this is his last birthday and you missed it for no good reason," my mother said. I did think about it and realized I was crazy to be missing important things in my life because of exercise.*
> —Kristin

Another clue is when someone has an unrealistic idea of what *not* exercising will do to the body. Compulsive exercisers are afraid that if they miss one workout, their muscles will atrophy and anything they eat will instantly turn to fat.

Compulsive exercisers also no longer enjoy

working out. They aren't doing it because it makes them feel healthier and more energetic. Rather, they are doing it because they feel they have no choice. They work out even if they have injuries or feel sick. An exercise addict will run with stress fractures, go to the gym with a sore throat, and miss sleep in order to get an extra workout.

Another sign that exercise has become an addiction is when someone starts to lie about how much he or she exercises. One compulsive exerciser belonged to three gyms so that no one would see how much time she spent working out. Another ran before anyone else in her family was awake so they would not know she did a morning workout in addition to the hour and a half she worked out after school. Laura, a high school sophomore, kept her exercising secret for almost a year.

> *I arranged my classes so I had study hall at the end of the day, then asked permission to leave early. I told my teachers that I had to watch my little brother after school and it would help if I had the extra time to pick him up. It was a big, fat lie. At school, I would change into running clothes, then run the five miles home. Then I would do a series of sit-ups and push-ups. Right before my mom was expected home (with my little brother), I would take a quick shower, then change back into my school clothes. After she got home, I'd casually say that I was going for a quick run, then do the whole routine again. She would have worried if she knew my entire evening was taken up by exercise and I didn't want to deal with it.*

## POSSIBLE SIGNS OF EXERCISE ADDICTION

⊙ Exercising every day, even if injured or sick

⊙ Avoiding friends or family because of the exercise routine

⊙ Being afraid of getting fat if a workout is missed

⊙ Becoming depressed if a workout is missed

⊙ Deciding how much to exercise based on what was eaten that day

⊙ Lying about how much time is spent exercising

⊙ Thinking constantly of ways to burn calories

## POSSIBLE SIGNS OF MUSCLE DYSMORPHIA

⊙ Eating a large amount of food to bulk up

⊙ Taking dietary supplements or steroids

⊙ Being afraid of losing muscle mass if one workout is missed

⊙ Lying about how much time is spent at the gym

⊙ Basing self-worth on body size

⊙ Allowing workouts to affect social and private life

# WHAT ARE THE EFFECTS OF COMPULSIVE EXERCISING?

There is no question that moderate exercising is good for you. Studies have shown that exercise reduces the chance of heart disease, high blood pressure, and some forms of cancer. Exercise also strengthens the immune system, which fights against disease and infection. People who exercise regularly sleep better, have more energy, and are better able to deal with stress. It can also have positive psychological effects such as building confidence, learning to work as a member of a team, and becoming more assertive.

With all these positive benefits, it can be hard to believe that exercise is sometimes dangerous. However, when taken to an extreme, the bad qualities of exercise overshadow the good ones. People who exercise too much become injured easily. Stress fractures, pulled muscles, and torn ligaments are quite common. And because compulsive exercisers do not slow down when they have an injury, the condition usually becomes worse. Permanent damage or the need for surgery is often the result.

Because they are burning so many more calories than they are consuming, compulsive exercisers become weak and tired. Their immune system breaks down and they get infections very easily. If they continue to push themselves, they may end up in the hospital because of severe dehydration or illness.

In addition, people with muscle dysmorphia often use anabolic steroids or performance-enhancing drugs to get the results they want.

These have many serious side effects, including violent, irrational behavior and impotence.

Compulsive exercising also takes a great emotional toll. People begin to push away their friends and families because of their need to work out. They become more and more isolated as the condition worsens. As a result, their self-perceptions become very distorted. They can no longer look at themselves and their bodies realistically.

# WHAT IS THE FEMALE ATHLETE TRIAD?

Young women who participate in athletics or suffer from compulsive exercising are at risk for a serious condition called the female athlete triad. The triad was first recognized in 1992 by the American College of Sports Medicine. It is comprised of three interrelated conditions.

## Condition One: Disordered Eating

Many athletes try to control their weight by controlling their eating habits. Disordered eating does not necessarily involve the extremes of anorexia or bulimia. It can be as simple as poor nutrition and the lack of essential vitamins and minerals. The incidence of eating disorders is much higher for athletes than the general population. One study indicates that 4.2 percent of female college athletes have anorexia and 39.2 percent have bulimia. Estimates of disordered eating are as high as 60 percent.

## Condition Two: Amenorrhea

The second condition is amenorrhea, meaning the loss of one's period or an irregular menstrual cycle. Amenorrhea is necessary for the diagnosis of anorexia, but any pattern of disordered eating can result in it. Experts believe that when a woman takes in fewer calories than she is expending, the production of estrogen is slowed, leading to the loss of menstruation.

Extremely low body fat percentages are also a cause. Once a woman's body fat level drops below 17 percent, she stops menstruating. More than 50 percent of the young women who participate in activities such as running, gymnastics, and dance suffer from amenorrhea.

## Condition Three: Osteoporosis

The last condition is osteoporosis, or brittle bone disease. Typically, osteoporosis doesn't affect women until after menopause, but doctors are now seeing teenagers with the bones of sixty-year-old women. Osteoporosis occurs when the body does not absorb enough calcium to maintain healthy, strong bones. The lack of estrogen that results from disordered eating and amenorrhea leads directly to this condition. The result of osteoporosis is stress fractures and broken bones.

Although many young women, especially those involved in sports that emphasize appearance or size, believe that extreme training and rigid diets are the way to achieve success, they couldn't be more wrong. Most women with female athlete triad do not have the stamina to be great athletes.

*I started cross-country as a freshman. My best friend was on the team and convinced me to join. I loved it. I couldn't believe how good I felt after a tough workout. I lost a few pounds and developed muscle tone. I guess my love for the sport made me a little obsessed. I began to run in the morning in addition to the team workouts after school. I never took a day off. I would spend hours every weekend running and did endless sets of sit-ups and push-ups to make myself stronger.*

*The first few seasons were great. I continued to improve and made varsity my sophomore year. But at the end of my junior year, things started to get bad. I had been restricting my food intake while I continued the strenuous workouts. I thought losing more weight would make me even faster. Boy, was I wrong! Instead I became weaker and my times slowed. I went to the doctor because my shins were killing me and he discovered that I had five stress fractures and extremely brittle bones. I had to drop out of cross-country to let my legs heal. At that point, I didn't have the strength to race anyway.*

—Jessica

## IS IT POSSIBLE TO RECOVER FROM EXERCISE COMPULSION?

Unfortunately, it often takes a serious injury for people to realize how much damage compulsive exercising and muscle dysmorphia can do. Only when people with these disorders are forced to cut back do they realize how much their bodies and social lives have suffered. Some of the side effects, such as osteoporosis and damage due to steroids, may be long-lasting problems.

It is possible to turn things around before this point is reached. However, as with anorexia, bulimia, and binge eating disorder, it is difficult to recover from exercise compulsion and muscle dysmorphia without professional help. People with these disorders need to reframe the way they view themselves and explore the deeper issues that underlie the compulsion.

# Part

## 2

# Understanding Types of Support

# 6

# Asking for Support

*I* *knew deep down that what I was doing was damaging, but I didn't have the courage to tell anyone or the strength to stop. One day, my school had an assembly about eating disorders. One of the speakers was a girl who had suffered from severe bulimia for about ten years. She almost died from heart failure because her electrolyte levels were so messed up. When she told her story, it seemed like she was talking directly to me. I had tears streaming down my face the whole time. She had done many of the same things I was doing.*

*The fact that she came so close to dying, and the fact that she had survived and was now living a normal life, made me want to get help. After the assembly, the school arranged it so people could talk to the speakers in private. I went in to see her and started sobbing right away. I couldn't say a word, but she knew exactly what the problem was. Right there she called a hotline and I talked to one of the counselors who gave me the names of therapists in my area.*

*It has now been two years since that day. Though I still have problems with food, I am much, much better and improving more every day.*
—Ramona

If you recognize yourself or someone you know in the descriptions of the various eating disorders in the previous section, you now need information regarding the different forms of support that are available. The following sections discuss the numerous treatment options, types of therapy, support groups, and the professionals that should be involved every step of the way. Recovery is not easy, but if you are well informed and know all the options, it will seem less daunting.

## THE NEXT STEP

Admitting that you have an eating disorder is not easy. Many individuals with eating disorders tend not to see their conditions as critical, even when people tell them that they need help. For others, the most difficult part is getting over the shame and guilt they feel about their behavior. If you are able to acknowledge that you have a problem with food and weight, you have taken a very difficult and important step.

However, it is not enough to simply recognize that you have an eating disorder. You must take the next step and begin the recovery process. Statistics show that treatment is more successful for those who initiate it themselves. When you enter treatment willingly, it means that you are ready to confront the problems and deal with the consequences. You are dedicated to focusing on your health instead of on the disordered behaviors. There is a certain amount of power in deciding that the eating disorder isn't going to be a part of your future.

If you don't seek help on your own, a loved one may have to put you in treatment, depending on the severity of your case. If someone else starts the recovery process, it can be very frightening. You may feel resentful and that you have lost control. As a result, treatment will be less successful and take much longer.

To begin recovering from the disorder, you need to talk to others and ask for support. Remember that it is nearly impossible to fight an eating disorder alone. Trying to handle all your problems on your own is a large part of what led you to the disorder in the first place. You need to break out of the isolation that the eating disorder has placed you in and learn to trust people.

Support comes in many different forms. It may be a friend who sits with you during lunch, a school counselor you can check in with throughout the day, a group of strangers with the same disorder, or a professional therapist to help you change your perspective.

Right now, the thought of all those people entering your life is probably pretty scary. Remember that recovery is a long process with many stages. Unless your condition is critical, you can take your time telling people. You may start by talking to your parents and seeing a therapist, then telling a few close friends. Later, when you are more comfortable, you can tell your teachers, school administrators, and anyone else.

*When I started going to a therapist for anorexia, I didn't want anyone at school to know. I thought they would laugh and always be staring at me. I didn't want to be labeled as "the girl with the eating disorder." But finally, after a few months of therapy, I told my best friend. I was scared when I told her, but she was great. She has been the biggest help ever. She always sits with me at lunch and talks about all kinds of things when I eat so I don't think about all the food that is going into my stomach. Soon, I think I am going to tell more friends. I am starting to realize that being open with people and getting their support is really important.*
—Danielle

You may find during the course of your recovery that some people are not able to fully support you. Your new ways of dealing with issues may alienate them or make them uncomfortable. If this happens, it is not your fault. They may be suffering from their own problems that they are not ready to confront. It is best not to depend on them and to surround yourself with other people who are more supportive.

*For the past five years, I was a compulsive eater. I was overweight and tended to be friends with people who were also overweight. One day, I got fed up with feeling out of control and unhappy, so I went to an Overeaters Anonymous meeting. It was exactly what I needed. I realized that I was burying my feelings in food and I learned healthier ways to cope. As a result, I began to lose weight. I no longer felt the need to take candy bar breaks during the day and no longer wanted to go to the all-you-can-eat buffets with my friends.*

*Most people were happy for me and very supportive. But one friend, Rita, started acting really strange. She kept trying to get me to eat with her. She would constantly offer me cookies and brownies. When I would say no, she became very angry. She said that I had changed and that I wasn't fun anymore. At first I was upset. I didn't want her not to like me. But after a while, I realized that she was making me feel bad about my progress. I began to hang out with her less and less. I can see now that our relationship was based on food and that we used each other to ease the shame of the binges.*

—Jean

## WHY IT MAY BE DIFFICULT TO ASK FOR HELP

There are many reasons that it may be difficult to tell somebody about your disorder and to ask for help. The main one is that the eating disorder, in a dangerous way, serves a purpose. It is a coping mechanism behind which you can hide from troubled thoughts and feelings. It has been protecting you from your problems. You may not want to give up the disordered behavior because you don't feel ready to face the deeper issues.

If you have had the eating disorder for a long time, the behavior may have become such a part of your daily routine that you can't imagine life without it. The thought of encountering food without all the rituals and disordered habits is probably very frightening. It may also be hard to deal with the free, unstructured time you will have once your day is no longer filled with thoughts about food. This was especially difficult for Debbie, who was recovering from bulimia. She always used to rush home after school to binge in the two hours that she had alone before her parents got home from work.

> When I first tried to give up my binges, those two hours were agony. I did anything I could to take my mind off food. I couldn't watch television because all the commercials for food drove me crazy. So I read and watched movies. I even started to crochet an afghan. My grandma showed me how. It became a lifesaver. I would think, "I just have to get to the end of this row." And then I would do another row. It kept me busy and stopped me from thinking about food.

Another reason it is difficult to ask for help is the issue of control. If your eating disorder is a way to assert control, it may be frightening to give that up for an unknown future. It may seem as if everyone who offers help is trying to take away your power and run your life.

Low self-esteem also makes it difficult to accept help. Often people with eating disorders feel that they don't have a right to their own needs. If you don't like yourself, you may not be able to see why someone would want to help you or why you should get better. Also, if you lack a strong sense of self, giving up the eating disorder can feel like giving up your identity.

All these reasons are extremely complex, and it takes a lot of courage to pull yourself away from that sort of thinking. It is hard to be completely honest with yourself and open up to others about things you want to keep private. However, if you want to begin recovering from the eating disorder, you need to talk to someone and get the necessary support.

## BREAKING FREE FROM ISOLATION

The decision about who to talk to first may be a difficult one. Do you feel comfortable going to your parents? If not, don't feel bad. Often it is hard to talk to immediate family members because they are so close to the situation—or may even be part of the problem.

Instead, it may be easier to talk to someone neutral, such as a family friend or a counselor at school. Or you may want to talk to a professional before confronting your friends and family. There are a number of organizations and hotlines that are set up for people seeking advice or information about eating disorders. Some of these are

**EATING DISORDERS AWARENESS
AND PREVENTION (EDAP)
INFORMATION AND
REFERRAL HOTLINE
(800) 931-2237**

EDAP is a great place to call if you have questions or want more information about eating disorders. The hotline is a confidential resource that is currently staffed from 8 AM to noon (Pacific time). Callers can leave a voicemail message twenty-four hours a day.

listed in the Where to Go for Help section at the back of this book. The people who staff the hotlines are trained to respond to issues surrounding eating disorders and will be able to give you advice and refer you to treatment centers and therapists in your area.

Besides who to tell, you should also decide when and where you tell people. Try to do it in a private place when you are all feeling calm. Maybe you want to talk to your mom when no one else is around, or maybe you would feel more comfortable telling your whole family at once. If you want to talk to a teacher or school counselor, you could ask to speak with him or her before or after class, or during a study period. Who and when you tell is a personal choice that depends on a lot of things. Do what makes you feel comfortable.

You are probably very nervous about talking to someone. This is completely normal. It may help to go over possible conversations in your head before you actually have them. Writing out what you want to say and practicing it is a great way to ease nervousness. Often, the opening phrase is the most difficult. If you don't know what to say, it is easy to avoid the conversation. You might use excuses like "Mom had a hard day at work. I don't want to upset her," or "Today just isn't the right day. Maybe tomorrow." If you have an opening phrase in your head, it will be easier to get past those excuses and just blurt it out. Some examples of possible lines are:

- ⊙ "I know you have been worried about me lately. I have a big problem and I want to talk with you about it."

- ⊙ "I've been having a lot of problems with food and dieting. I'm really scared and I think I might need help."

- ⊙ "I want to talk with you about something important. Can you promise to just listen and not get upset? This is really hard for me."

It may also help to envision people's reactions and plan your response. What will you do if they get upset or angry? What will you say if they don't think it is a big deal? Think about what the ideal reaction would be. Then imagine the worst-case scenario. If you are prepared for those two extremes, you will be able to handle anything that falls in between.

## TAKING CONTROL

The final thing you should do before talking to someone is to think about what the next step will be. If you don't have a clear sense of where you want to go from here, the process may seem more overwhelming. It is important that you think about what you want to happen next: Do you want to see a doctor, visit a therapist, or join a support group? Maybe you feel you need to go to a treatment center. But keep in mind that you are inviting others into the recovery process. They will definitely have opinions about what you should do. Often, when you are so entrenched in the eating disorder, it is hard to see all your options. It is important to listen to what others have to say and accept that maybe they see something you don't. Trust that they want what is best for you.

### COMMON QUESTIONS FROM THOSE ASKING FOR HELP

*Can I recover from an eating disorder?*
The answer is **yes.** Studies of people with anorexia who received treatment show that 50 to 70 percent no long suffer from clinical anorexia (they maintain a weight in the normal range and are menstruating), 25 percent show some symptoms (they are underweight and still have irregular periods), and the remaining 25 percent struggle with the condition.

Recovery from bulimia is more common. Statistics show a recovery rate of 50 percent. Relapse is common (about 30 percent within six years), but second recoveries are common as well. Rates of recovery from binge eating disorder, exercise compulsion, and muscle dysmorphia are even higher.

However, the road to recovery is long and there are many obstacles along the way. It will not be easy, but as long as you are committed to living a healthy life, there is no reason you should not be able to conquer your eating disorder.

### How long does it take to get better?

There is no one answer to this question. It takes different amounts of time for everyone. Experts have found that the length of time you have lived with your eating disorder is often an indication of how long treatment will take. If you are in the beginning stages, you may recover fairly quickly. If the eating disorder has been a part of your life for years, recovery will probably take longer.

Recovery also depends a great deal on your attitude. If you really want to recover and are willing to explore the reasons behind the disorder, even if they are very painful, your journey will be shorter. If you resist talking to professionals and won't try to learn new behaviors, it will take much longer and will be more difficult.

### Will I need professional help?
Because the disordered thought patterns are so deeply ingrained, it is extremely difficult to beat an eating disorder on your own. There are many professionals who are trained to help and support people with your problem. Let them help you. Different types of treatment and support groups will be discussed in the next chapters.

### Will I have to go to the hospital?
If your health is in jeopardy or you feel suicidal, hospitalization may be necessary. Many times, hospitalization is needed to stabilize weight. Studies have shown that people who are malnourished and/or starving cannot think clearly enough to enter therapy. When this is the case, maintaining a steady weight is essential before the process of recovery can begin.

### What if I don't always want to get better?
The reasons given earlier in this chapter for why it is difficult to ask for help won't disappear once you start treatment. You will struggle with them throughout the process of

recovery. Because an eating disorder is a coping mechanism, it is protecting you from feelings that are painful and difficult to deal with. When this is the case, it is common to be afraid to let go of the disorder. Just remember that your life without the eating disorder will be much more fulfilling than continuing to live with it.

***I admit that I have a problem and have asked for help. What is the next step?***
The next step is to decide on a course of treatment. It is important that you take an active role in the decisions. Young adults rarely get to choose their own doctors, especially when their parents foot the bill, so this may seem a little daunting. But if you don't feel comfortable with a certain therapist, recovery will be more difficult. There are many treatment options. It is important that you educate yourself about what is available in order to make the best choices. The next chapters will help.

# 7

# Support in Treatment

*The few days after I told my mom I needed help with my eating problems were a whirlwind. She spent hours on the phone. First she talked to all her friends and asked their advice. Then she called a few different eating disorder organizations and got referrals from them. Then she talked to people at different clinics and hospitals and found out about the different programs. The entire time, she told me everything she learned. For some of the calls, I even listened on the other extension. At first I thought she was crazy and taking things way too far. But I have to admit that all the research paid off. We found a therapist whom I like a lot and who is helping me recover.*
—Suzannah

When looking at treatment options, the most important thing to keep in mind is that they are not all the same. Different experts have different views about the causes of eating disorders, hence they

91

have different approaches to treatment. Although this variety may seem overwhelming, it is actually a very good thing. Because there are so many choices, it is possible to find a course of treatment that works well with your personality and lifestyle.

In order to find the right place for you, you need to know something about the various types of centers, the kinds of professionals who should be involved, and the different approaches to therapy. Then you should talk to people in a number of different clinics, hospitals, and centers and learn as much as you can about them and their forms of treatment. Remember that the professionals should work with you. You should not try to hide or change your feelings to fit with a type of treatment that does not seem right for you and your family.

No matter what method of treatment you choose, there should be three major aims:

1. To make you healthy and ensure survival
2. To help you understand the issues beyond the problems with food and weight
3. To teach you new ways of coping with these issues

## STRUCTURE OF TREATMENT

The first question to ask is how the treatment should be structured: Do you want it to be on an inpatient or outpatient basis? Many times, the choice depends upon the severity of your case, the area in which you live, and the type of insurance you carry. There are many advantages and disadvantages to both kinds of treatment programs.

# INPATIENT TREATMENT

Inpatient treatment means that you spend all day and all night in a medical or psychiatric facility. This around-the-clock care may be necessary if you have medical problems, such as malnutrition or severe electrolyte imbalances; if you deny that you need treatment; if you are suicidal; or if you live too far away from therapists for effective outpatient treatment.

### Pros

Some advantages to inpatient care are that it provides a structured setting and professionals are always available day or night. Medical conditions, food intake, and amount of exercise are easily monitored. Since the physicians, therapists, and nutritionists are a part of the same team, they work closely together and coordinate their efforts.

Therapy may be more effective during inpatient treatment because you'll be able to focus on the underlying issues while away from the daily pressures of family, school, and work. Many people think the more intensive therapy schedule is better than going once or twice a week as an outpatient. You can learn new behaviors and ways to solve problems in a safe environment with the constant support of others.

### Cons

One disadvantage to inpatient treatment is that it is very disruptive to your daily life. You will have to miss school and any other activities in which you are involved. You will not be able to see your friends and family every day. Going away also makes your disorder more public. People will wonder where you are and will need to be told.

Another disadvantage is that inpatient treatment is usually more expensive than outpatient treatment. Some types of insurance will cover only a certain number of days at an inpatient center or require that treatment be obtained at a specific hospital. It is important that you find out exactly what your insurance covers when researching different treatment options.

Residential treatment centers are becoming more and more prevalent. Such treatment centers offer twenty-four-hour care in a more relaxed setting than a hospital or clinic. They require that the patient is mentally and physically stable and does not have severe medical problems. Their goal is to make the transition to day-to-day life a little easier. Some even require that patients do volunteer projects or hold part-time jobs while at the center. Facilities vary a great deal in attitudes and level of care, so it is important to research each program thoroughly.

*My parents took me kicking and screaming to the treatment center at our local hospital. I didn't realize what a problem I had until the second week of therapy. It's been five years since I entered treatment and while I still have bad days, it is such a relief to be able to have a normal life that isn't totally dominated by food. I have been able to make new, wonderful friends and I feel stronger than I ever have before in my life. If I can conquer anorexia, I figure I can do just about anything!*
—Becky

## QUESTIONS TO ASK WHEN CONSIDERING INPATIENT TREATMENT

⊙ Are only people with eating disorders treated, or will you be with people suffering from other problems, such as depression, chemical abuse, mood disorders, etc.?

⊙ What are the ages of most patients? Will you be the only young person in a group of adults?

⊙ How flexible is the program about the length of time you can stay? Is there a set number of days for treatment? What happens if you are not ready to leave at that time?

⊙ What is the daily schedule like?

⊙ What are the goals of the therapy?

⊙ What kind of follow-up is available? Does the center offer support groups and/or outpatient therapy?

⊙ What are the credentials of all the therapists and staff?

⊙ How long has the program been around? How many patients with your disorder have been treated at the center?

## Outpatient Treatment

Because of the high costs associated with inpatient treatment and the lack of eating disorder centers in many areas, the majority of treatment is done on an outpatient basis. There is a wide range of types of outpatient treatments available. An outpatient program may be offered by centers that do inpatient treatment, or at eating disorder clinics or mental health care facilities. As with inpatient programs, outpatient facilities vary a great deal in philosophy and level of care, so it is important to do a lot of research before selecting one.

If you feel that you don't need twenty-four-hour care, but you want more structure than simply seeing a therapist a few times a week, partial hospitalization or day treatment could be an option. There are many different programs available. Some have sessions a few days a week, whereas others have you in treatment all day every day, then send you home at night.

### Pros

This type of treatment is often less disruptive to daily life. Depending on the schedule, you may be able to go to school part-time and continue to participate in some activities. Another advantage is that you can incorporate the strategies you learn into your real life right away while receiving constant support and care. For this reason, it is often used as a transition for patients who have just finished inpatient treatment but still don't feel ready to confront life on their own.

Many people receive care by seeing an individual therapist. Depending on your needs, you might see the therapist as often as several times a week or as infrequently as once a month. If you have had your eating disorder for a relatively short amount of time and are completely dedicated to getting better, you may not need the structure of other programs, and individual therapy may be a good option.

**Cons**
The lack of structure can also be seen as a disadvantage. It may take longer to develop trust in the therapist and open up about painful issues when you see him or her for only an hour once a week. Therefore, it is essential that you find a therapist you feel comfortable with and like.

The lack of a cohesive team in approaching recovery can also be a disadvantage of individual therapy. In treatment centers and clinics, therapists, physicians, and dietitians work together and consult with each other about patients in their care. If you see a separate therapist, nutritionist, and doctor, they won't know the areas that the others have covered and won't be able to build on things together. Additionally, they may have different philosophies about recovery that conflict, and this can make the process more difficult for you. It may be a good idea to ask a therapist if there is anyone with whom he or she works closely, or if he or she would be willing to consult with other professionals about your case.

## PROFESSIONALS INVOLVED IN TREATMENT

Whether you choose inpatient or outpatient treatment, there should be a team of professionals working with you on your recovery. Because eating disorders involve a complex combination of physical, emotional, and social factors, a comprehensive treatment plan should involve a variety of experts and approaches.

## Therapist

When you think of treatment for eating disorders, the first person you think of is probably the therapist. He or she plays a vital role in helping you realize why you have an eating disorder and showing you new strategies to deal with your problems.

There are many different philosophies therapists may have. One major difference between therapists is their attitude toward recovery from eating disorders. Some believe that you never fully recover—that you struggle with the disordered thoughts and behaviors for the rest of your life.

Others believe a total recovery is possible—that once you deal with the root issues and change your patterns of thinking, you can be completely free of the disordered thoughts and behaviors. This is an important distinction. If your goal is complete recovery and you have a therapist who doesn't feel that is possible, you are bound to have problems. Similarly, if you feel you will struggle with the eating disorder for the rest of your life and your therapist is aiming for a full recovery, it will be difficult to get what you want from treatment.

Another difference is in the types of therapy practiced by professionals. Two common approaches are psychoanalytic therapy and cognitive-behavioral therapy. One has not been proven better than the other in treating eating disorders. Success depends entirely on the patient and is impossible to predict.

## Psychoanalytic Therapy

In psychoanalytic therapy, you delve into the underlying issues that caused you to develop an eating disorder. This involves talking about your past experiences in order to understand your behavior in the present. Possible subjects of discussion include self-esteem; your opinions on the social ideal of thinness; loneliness; and the need for attention, power, and control.

Professionals who use this model see the disordered behavior as an adaptive function that protects you against pain and fear. They believe that without addressing the underlying reasons for the disorder, the symptoms may stop temporarily but will either reappear or manifest themselves in another way.

One difficulty with this approach is that if someone is extremely starved, depressed, or compulsive, he or she will not be able to think clearly enough to make the therapy effective. Critics of psychotherapy also argue that sufferers can talk about their problems for years while still practicing the disordered behavior. These critics promote a method of treatment that addresses both thinking and behavior—cognitive behavioral therapy.

## Cognitive Behavioral Therapy

Cognitive behavioral therapy is based on the belief that a person with an eating disorder has distorted perceptions regarding food and weight that lead to disordered behavior. The therapy revolves around changing the patient's perceptions, then changing his or her behaviors. Past events and feelings are not discussed in great detail. Instead, the focus is on how the person thinks and acts in the present.

Common faulty thought patterns in eating disorder patients include magical thinking (such as when someone with anorexia believes she'll be happy once she loses ten pounds); magnifying; all-or-nothing thinking (such as when a binge eater consumes an entire bag of cookies because she believes that she has already ruined the entire day by eating one); and overgeneralizing (such as when someone with bulimia thinks that she will get fat if she doesn't purge).

Once the patients understand that this type of thinking is distorted, they can begin to change their behavior. After someone with anorexia realizes that losing ten pounds won't magically make her happy, she can see how extreme dieting won't solve all her problems. When a binge eater realizes that cookies are not "bad" and that they can be incorporated into a healthy meal plan, she will be less likely to binge. And once someone with bulimia understands that eating without purging does not automatically lead to weight gain, she can begin to remove purging from her life.

## Stages of Therapy

No matter what framework a therapist uses, therapy can be seen as having a definite course with a beginning, middle, and end. There is no set time limit on each stage. Some people may have more problems with one area than others, which results in different lengths of time in each stage.

The *Journal of Consulting and Clinical Psychology* lists four components that need to be present for successful therapy:

⊙ There should be a clear understanding of the goals and aims of therapy, the role of the therapist, your responsibility, and the expected time frame of treatment.

⊙ The therapy should give you skills that you can use immediately to control your life in a healthy way.

⊙ The therapist should emphasize that you learn to use these skills independently of him or her.

⊙ The therapist should encourage you to see that progress is due to you and your actions, not the therapist.

## Phase I

Because people with eating disorders have a hard time trusting people and building intimate relationships, the first stage of therapy is devoted to establishing trust between the therapist and the patient. It is also the time when patients learn to describe their emotions. This can be very difficult because people with eating disorders often use the disorder to avoid their true feelings, so they don't know how to express them. As trust and the ability to describe their emotional state increase, the patient is ready to begin the middle stage.

### Phase II

The middle phase of therapy is the most difficult. In psychoanalytic therapy, it is when the patient recognizes the causes of tension in her life and the factors that drove her to an eating disorder. Feelings that have been deeply buried are discussed. New roles in relationships are worked out and new ways to cope with conflict are discovered. In cognitive behavioral therapy, the middle stage is when faulty thought patterns are changed and new behaviors are learned. As these new skills replace the disordered behaviors, the patient is ready to enter the last stage.

### Phase III

The final stage is when the patient transfers the coping skills she has learned in therapy to her real life without the help of the therapist. It is common for some symptoms of the eating disorder to return as the patient realizes the uncertainty of life without therapy. But if the patient is truly ready to end therapy, she should have the confidence and trust in herself to move forward in a healthy way.

## Finding a Therapist

There are many ways to go about finding a therapist. First, you could call some of the organizations in the back of this book. All of them will gladly send you lists of therapists in your area. Second is to ask your school nurse or physician for a referral. They may have dealt with this issue before and be famil-iar with people in the field. The yellow pages or local psychological referral services also provide names of therapists. However, this is a somewhat risky way to go. Anyone can get a listing, so you need to do a more thorough background check.

The most important thing about finding a thera-pist is that you feel comfortable with that person. It doesn't matter how many degrees the therapist has or how many patients he or she has treated if you feel uneasy. People have a tendency to trust author-ity figures. If things aren't working out, they blame themselves instead of the expert. Remember, thera-pists are people with distinct personalities. Just as there are some people you find difficult to get along with, there will be therapists you won't like. If you find it hard to trust the therapist, you won't be able to open up and honestly discuss important issues. However, it is important not to use this as an excuse. The therapist will make you talk about some deep and possibly painful feelings. While this may make you uncomfortable, it is not a reason to stop seeing that person.

## Physician

Before you start any type of treatment program, you should be evaluated by a physician. The doctor will be able to find any problems associated with starva-tion, bingeing, purging, or excessive exercising. In someone with anorexia, a doctor should look for low blood pressure, slow heartbeat, reduced thyroid metabolism, changes in electrocardiogram (ECG), and a lowered white blood cell count. In a person suffering from bulimia, the doctor might find swollen

## QUESTIONS TO ASK WHEN SELECTING A THERAPIST

⊙ How long have you been treating eating disorders?

⊙ How many patients have you seen with my type of problem?

⊙ How long does therapy usually last?

⊙ What happens during the course of the treatment?

⊙ How does a typical session with you go?

⊙ What are your goals for therapy?

⊙ What are your feelings about medication?

⊙ What kind of follow-up care is available after therapy ends?

glands, ulcers in the esophagus and stomach, tears in the throat, electrolyte abnormalities, and dysfunctional bowels. Compulsive overeaters may have high blood pressure or high cholesterol that need to be monitored. Compulsive exercisers often have stress fractures, joint problems, and malnutrition. All of these problems are generally treatable, but they can be deadly without proper monitoring.

Throughout the treatment process, physical examinations should take place frequently. The eating disorder has affected your body, and your condition needs to be watched as you move toward recovery. Most of the health problems should improve during treatment, but some may not. Only a doctor can tell you your prognosis.

## Psychiatrist

A psychiatrist is a doctor who practices psychotherapy and is an authority on drug therapy. As we have seen in the earlier chapters, many experts believe that there are biological reasons for some eating disorders. When this is the case, drugs can often relieve some symptoms. However, many professionals are hesitant to prescribe drugs until other options have been tried. Most often, drugs are used to reduce anxiety, to help normalize the thinking process, and when other psychiatric conditions exist, such as depression or obsessive-compulsive disorder. Due to the possible side effects of drugs, psychiatrists should work closely with any other professionals you are seeing.

## Dietitian/Nutritionist

It may seem strange that someone as focused on food as a person with an eating disorder needs a nutritionist. Don't they already know the amount of fat and calories in every kind of food anyway? Although eating disorder victims often know a great deal about some aspects of nutrition, they usually also have many misconceptions and negative attitudes toward healthy foods. A nutritionist will teach you about a good, balanced diet; how your body uses food; and what the benefits of a varied diet are, and will answer any questions you might have. A dietitian will show you the truth about many misconceptions. For example, someone told Jenny, who suffered from anorexia, that bananas have more calories than other fruit, so Jenny labeled them as a "bad" food and totally eliminated them from her diet. She thought that if she ate a banana she would automatically gain weight. A nutritionist put bananas into perspective for her and pointed out the many good nutrients, such as potassium, that bananas contain.

The same care should be given to finding a good nutritionist as to choosing a therapist. The term "nutritionist" can be used by anyone and does not necessarily indicate a particular level of training or experience. A licensed registered dietitian is a safe bet because you know that the person has a four-year college degree in nutrition and dietetics, has completed an internship, and has passed the American Dietetic Association's test for registration. However, not all dietitians are trained to work with eating disorder patients, so it is important to ask about experience.

# 8 Support Groups

*E*ven though my therapist played a huge role in my recovery, I found the support group to be almost more beneficial. The group was led by a professional (not my own therapist) and included eight other people with bulimia. It really opened my eyes to hear them tell their stories. For so long I thought I was the only one in the world bingeing and purging. My family tried to understand, but they really couldn't. It was great to talk to people who were going through the same thing. At times it was hard, though. The girls in the group could see right through the lies I told everyone else. They made me admit some things I was afraid to tell anyone. While talking about these issues is scary, it is also the best thing in the world.
—Geena

In addition to the professional help necessary for recovery from an eating disorder, support groups are essential. In support groups, people with the same or similar problems get together to discuss the problem. Support groups can be a part of therapy with an expert, or they can be discovered on your own. They exist in every part of the country,and can be found at hospitals, college campuses, community centers, and on the Internet. You can even start one yourself.

## GROUP THERAPY

In group therapy, people meet in a supportive setting with a qualified professional to learn through sharing, supporting, and giving feedback to the other people in the group. A group might learn communication skills, recognize self-defeating behaviors, and learn strategies for changing. Group therapy is usually used in conjunction with individual therapy—either at the same time or as follow-up or maintenance. In general, it has been found that group therapy is more effective for people with bulimia and binge eating disorders than for those with anorexia. This could be because people suffering from anorexia tend to be more withdrawn and anxious and have more problems expressing their feelings.

One of the biggest benefits of group therapy is that the patient sees that she is not the only one with the problem. Often people with eating disorders feel isolated, alone, and misunderstood. Groups provide a safe place to explore your feelings without worrying about being judged. They are also a place to learn how to create intimate relationships. You can talk to others who have made the same commitment to recovery and learn from their experiences. Often something stated by a peer is more effective than if it comes from an authority figure. It may also help to be in contact with people in similar situations who are making progress. Many in group therapy learn to believe, "If she can do it, so can I."

There are many types of groups available. Some are closed, which means that the same members meet every time and that the group is not open to new members. These groups tend to meet for a specific amount of time, such as six months. Other groups are open, meaning that new members can join at any time. They tend to meet for indefinite periods of time, with older members dropping out and new members constantly joining.

The groups can also be structured or unstructured. Structured groups have set agendas and topics for discussion and follow a certain format. Unstructured groups talk about anything at any time. You can also choose between groups of people with your same problem, or groups of people with different, but related, problems.

It is important to remember that not all groups are beneficial for everyone. It may take a few session to learn if a group is right for you. If the leader is not properly trained or doesn't have enough experience with eating disorders, the group may not be very helpful. It is important to check out the therapist's training and credentials before joining a group. You also want to make sure you feel comfortable with the people in the group. Although it is natural to have some reservations at first, if you feel attacked, belittled, or very uncomfortable, you should find a different group.

A group may have a negative impact if the members want to talk about ways of maintaining their disorders instead of learning new ways of coping. For example, some groups of people with anorexia may want to learn new methods of hiding food or ways to burn extra calories, or groups of individuals suffering from bulimia may try to learn new ways of purging. Another concern is that patients often feel the eating disorder increases their self-worth, so they start competing with others.

A good group will help you decrease disordered behavior, not learn new ways to promote it. In a group, you should feel hopeful and positive. If a group is focused only on the negative aspects of your situation and is pessimistic, it won't be beneficial.

## FAMILY SUPPORT AND THERAPY

As we have seen, family dynamics often play a role in the development and maintenance of eating disorders. Because of this, family therapy is an important tool in the recovery process. Therapy is also a good way to educate all family members about eating disorders. It is a time when questions can be answered by qualified professionals.

In therapy, family members learn how their behaviors may have contributed to your eating disorder. Expectations and pressures are explored. Boundaries and rules are examined. The goal is to teach family members new ways of acting and thinking that are healthier than their current patterns.

In family therapy, Melissa was able to confront her father for the first time about how painful it was when he teased her about her baby fat. "He had never realized how much I took those comments to heart and how they really made me feel unattractive. He felt that it was just good-natured teasing and that it was just his way of showing affection. Now I can see that he is more careful about the things he says to me and my little sister."

In a family with an eating disorder, there are often other problems as well. Depression, alcoholism, and abuse are all examples of common issues that such families deal with. Therapy often exposes deeper issues and how they influence and affect the behavior of different family members.

## SELF-HELP GROUPS

Self-help groups are similar to group therapy, except that they are run by the members of the group, not a trained professional. The idea is that a person experiencing a problem is the best support and help for someone else with that same problem. A group member will get support from the other members while also providing support to others. A self-help group should not be the only form of treatment, but it is an excellent way to find additional support.

The same benefits and potential problems exist with self-help groups as with group therapy. The benefits include reducing feelings of isolation and loneliness, finding acceptance and support, getting information and suggestions from people who have "been there," and finding good role models in people who are recovering. Some potential problems are reinforcement of disordered behavior, competition for who has the "worst" case, and the lack of professional guidance.

## Starting Your Own Self-Help Group

If you live in an area where there are no support groups, or if you don't feel comfortable in the ones that are available, you may want to form your own group. Tracy, a high school junior, decided to start a support group after meeting another person recovering from anorexia during lunch in the school cafeteria.

> *I sat across from a girl I really didn't know. She had a tuna sandwich that she just kept staring at. Somehow I knew exactly what was going through her head. Although I had been through a treatment program, I sometimes still feel afraid to take that first bite. We started talking and it turned out that she did have anorexia and was seeing a therapist three times a week. We started eating lunch together every day and talking on the phone whenever things got tough. Having someone who knew what I was going through helped so much. We decided to ask other girls we knew who were having food problems if they wanted to have meetings. A guidance counselor gave us her room to use, and every week we met and just talked about things. Soon, we had a group of about six regular people, although other people would drop in once in a while.*

**HERE ARE A FEW QUESTIONS TO KEEP IN MIND AS YOU LOOK FOR MEMBERS AND ORGANIZE THE FIRST MEETING:**

⊙ Will the group be only for people with eating disorders or do you want family members and friends to also attend?

⊙ Will the group be all girls or would you allow boys to join?

⊙ Do you want all the members to be teenagers?

⊙ What is the maximum number of people you would allow to join? For good group discussions, ten is usually the maximum number if you want full participation from all members.

⊙ Do you want to charge dues to help pay for supplies?

⊙ Will you invite speakers to give presentations? Will you pay or ask them to volunteer?

To find members, you can ask teachers and counselors, doctors, therapists, hospitals, and clergy members if they know anyone who would benefit from such a group. You could also put up signs in school restrooms or locker rooms. Keep in mind that it may take a while to get people to sign up. Even if you have only one or two other people, you should still start the group.

Once you have a list of people who are interested in the group, you should set up the first meeting. Meeting places can be at churches, YMCAs, schools, or community centers. If you know the people in the group, you could meet at someone's house. However, this sometimes puts pressure on the host and can be uncomfortable if the group is large and includes people you don't know well.

At the first meeting, you should decide on the structure of the group. Do you want someone to be the group leader? Do you want to have specific issues to talk about at each meeting or do you want to have open conversations with no themes? Tracy's group had no set agenda for the first few meetings.

*It didn't really work well. We either talked about the same things over and over, or we got off track and would talk about our favorite TV shows or gossip about people at school. So we decided to have a different person lead each week's discussion. We made up a list of topics we thought were important, like how to handle stress, how to deal with comments from people who don't understand the disorder, how to deal with family. Each meeting one person would develop questions and do research on the topic. That way the meetings were much more productive.*

You should also determine rules and guidelines at the first meeting. A few specific rules will help keep the meetings on target and ensure that all members respect the aims and goals of the group. Examples of some possible rules are:

⊙ Keep anything said during the meeting confidential. The only exception to this is if someone seems suicidal or her health is in danger.

⊙ Never talk when someone else is talking.

⊙ Listen carefully to what others are saying.

⊙ Respect differences in opinion.

⊙ Make working toward recovery the main goal. Don't let the group become a forum for maintaining disordered behavior.

⊙ Make sure everyone is given the opportunity to contribute to the group. If people don't feel like they are making an impact on the group, they won't stay in it.

## ON-LINE SUPPORT

If you have access to the Internet, it has many sources of valuable information and support. Many on-line services, such as AOL, have chat rooms for members. You can find chat rooms for all eating disorders and all ages. They are either run at certain times during the week with discussion topics and leaders, or they can operate twenty-four hours a day, seven days a week as a place to express your thoughts and feelings. Bulletin boards are places on-line where people can post messages that others read and respond to. Many organizations have Web sites to educate people about eating disorders. Check the back of this book for some sites that are valuable sources of information.

The anonymity you receive on-line is helpful for people who think they may have an eating disorder but are not yet ready to commit to therapy. They can talk to other people about their recovery process and gather the courage to confront their own personal issues. It is a place to observe and listen to people as they learn about and confront their eating disorders. In a chat room, you can have people respond to your questions and fears.

Once you have begun the recovery process, you can use on-line sources to reflect on your progress and help others as they go through the same issues. It can be very rewarding to help someone who is just beginning to confront her problems.

Jodie found on-line chat rooms incredibly helpful during her first semester at college. The stress and uncertainty of being away from home for the first time was making her bulimia worse. The school offered an eating disorders support group, but Jodie didn't feel comfortable going to it. She was trying to make friends and was afraid of what they would think if they learned that she had bulimia. She found a chat room for college-age women with bulimia and soon was conversing several times a day with people in her situation. With the support and understanding she got from the group, she was able to get up enough courage to tell her roommate about her eating disorder and to join the support group at her school.

You should remember that some of the good points about on-line services also make them dangerous. Be wary of giving out any personal information, and don't believe everything you hear.

## TWELVE-STEP PROGRAMS

Twelve-step programs view eating disorders as addictions or diseases. The best known twelve-step program for eating disorders, Overeaters Anonymous, is based upon the Alcoholics Anonymous (AA) model. AA considers alcoholism an addiction and believes that alcoholics are powerless over alcohol because of the way their bodies react to it. In the basic literature for Overeaters Anonymous, the word "alcohol" is replaced with "food." The group uses the same twelve steps and traditions as AA. It stresses spirituality and asks participants to give control to a "higher power."

People who are compulsive eaters typically feel guilty, powerless, and depressed about their behavior. They believe that they should have better control over what they eat, and the popularity of diets and weight-loss schemes promotes this thinking. In OA, the first step is for someone to admit that she cannot control what she eats because she is addicted to food and a compulsive eater. Food is seen as a "drug" that makes its victims powerless.

The twelve-step groups focus on behavioral changes that help addicted individuals through their daily lives. There are strict requirements in OA— you must limit yourself to three meals a day, restrict the types of food at each meal, check in with your sponsor, and attend OA meetings regularly. The organization also promotes abstinence from certain foods that are considered triggers for binges, such as sugar and white flour.

For many people with bulimia and binge eating disorder, these requirements are comforting and helpful. OA meetings are held in all parts of the country, day and night. Having a sponsor whom you can call at three o'clock in the morning when you feel like bingeing is a tremendous form of support. In addition, the meetings focus more on group interaction than on the individual person, which helps some people feel less isolated.

For others, however, the focus on food increases eating disordered thoughts and behaviors. Most experts feel that people with anorexia should not take part in twelve-step programs because abstinence from food should never be a part of the recovery process for those with anorexia, no matter what that food is. People with anorexia are already abstaining from food, and the OA focus promotes labeling some foods as good and others bad.

Critics feel that the abstinence requirement is tricky with any eating disorder. A person cannot not eat, like an alcoholic can abstain completely from drinking. Dealing with food cannot be a black-and-white issue, like dealing with drugs. People need to eat every day. Therefore, many people feel that the goal of recovery should be to be able to deal with all food in a healthy way.

Labeling certain foods as addictive can maintain disordered thinking about food.

Another criticism is that in the addiction model of treatment, one is never fully recovered. If a person no longer practices disordered behavior, he or she is considered in remission, but he or she still has the disorder. Someone with bulimia who has not binged and purged for ten years must still refer to herself as having bulimia and attend OA meetings.

*When I was a freshman in high school I started dating a junior. I had a great time hanging out with his friends and doing things like going to the prom. The only problem was that I stopped hanging out with people in my grade. The next year, after he and all my friends graduated, I felt really abandoned and lonely. Then, to make things worse, the guy dumped me. I started comforting myself with extra treats and desserts. More and more I depended on food to numb my hurt feelings.*

*By the time it was my senior year I had gained almost thirty pounds. I was desperately unhappy. A friend of my mother's asked one day if I wanted to go with her to an Overeaters Anonymous meeting. At first I said no. I thought it would be a bunch of fat old ladies moaning about how horrible their lives were. But as I became more and more unhappy with myself, I finally decided to go to one meeting. It wasn't like I had imagined at all. Everyone was really nice and there were even some young people there.*

*I kept going to the meetings and hooked up with a sponsor whom I could call whenever I felt like bingeing or just wanted to talk. Trying to avoid certain foods has helped, too. Now I don't feel the intense cravings I used to have. With this strong support system behind me, I am finally losing the extra weight.*
—Barbara

# 9 Supporting a Friend

**W**hen my sister was diagnosed with anorexia, it took over the family. Every meal revolved around whether or not she was eating. We begged her to eat, then tried to bribe her, then yelled at her. Nothing worked.

After she had been in therapy for a few weeks, the entire family went to a session. The therapist told us that what we had been doing was the wrong way to help. When he explained it, we could see how our actions were actually doing more harm than good. We got some good guidelines and tried to follow them as closely as possible. It's hard though. Most people don't realize that it's not only the person with the disorder who suffers. Friends and family members suffer, too.

—Donna

When a friend or family member has an eating disorder, it is devastating. Suddenly things you took for granted become very difficult. Mealtimes are a battlefield, social events get disrupted, and relationships shift dramatically.

The personality of someone with an eating disorder changes as well. Many parents report feeling shocked when their usually calm, good, obedient daughter suddenly becomes stubborn, uncompromising, and secretive. Friends say that once-social people become very withdrawn and distant.

It is very hard to know how to act or what to say when a friend develops an eating disorder. It is even harder if you want to confront them about it.

## HOW TO APPROACH A FRIEND ABOUT AN EATING DISORDER

If you think a friend has an eating disorder, it may be difficult to talk with her about it. There are a few steps you can take to help things go more smoothly.

First of all, learn all you can about eating disorders before you talk with her. This way you can back up what you are telling her with facts and examples, and answer questions she may have. You might want to have some reading material on eating disorders that you can give her.

Next, pick a time when you know you won't be interrupted and a place where you'll have privacy. The discussion probably won't go as well if you are in a crowded restaurant where others may see you, or in your house when you can hear your family in the next room. Make sure you are able to give your undivided attention to your friend. Also, try to pick a time when you are both calm. If you know she had a stressful day at school or if you are really upset by something she did, don't bring it up immediately. When emotions are already high, it is difficult to have a clear conversation about something so serious.

When you open the conversation, try to use "I" statements instead of "you" statements. She will feel attacked and defensive if you say things like, "You never eat lunch. You must be anorexic." Instead, you should say, "I've noticed that you don't come to the cafeteria for lunch any more. I'm worried. Is anything wrong?"

Finally, try to convince her to get help. You can give her the names and numbers of the organizations in the back of this book, or get the names of therapists and support groups in your area to give to her. Or you could log onto an on-line support group with her and encourage her to participate or just read the postings of others. Don't pressure her too much, though. She may need some time to think it over.

When you confront your friend, she may deny the problem or downplay its seriousness. She may also get mad at you and tell you to mind your own business. If this happens, let her know that you are there for her, but that eating disorders are serious and that if she doesn't ask for help, you will have to tell others who can get her the treatment she needs.

## WHEN TO TELL OTHERS

It has been proven that treatment is more successful when the patient enters it willingly. However, many times people with eating disorders don't recognize how dangerous their behavior is and think that they don't need help. If this is the case, you may need to tell her parents or a teacher that you think she is in trouble. It is difficult to break a confidence, and you may feel as if you are betraying your friend's trust. But the reality is that if she has an eating disorder, you could be saving her life.

There are a few instances when you need to get immediate help no matter what the person says. If she has reached the point where she cannot function effectively due to starvation, bingeing, or purging; if she is unable to keep any food in her stomach without vomiting; if she seems suicidal; or if she is engaging in substance abuse or self-mutilation, she needs help right away.

*I had a feeling that my roommate at boarding school had an eating disorder. She never ate in the dining hall and became really withdrawn and sullen. She also started losing a ton of weight. I didn't tell anyone because I didn't think it was my place. Everybody has problems that they need to deal with on their own.*

*But I got worried when I heard people talk about how she fainted in class, or couldn't participate in gym because she was too weak. I confronted her, but she said everything was fine, she just had a nasty bout of the flu. But one morning, she couldn't get out of bed. It scared me so much that I called her parents, the school nurse, and the dorm supervisor. She was admitted to a hospital right away. I think she is really mad at me. She hasn't returned any of my phone calls or acknowledged the cards and flowers I sent. I'm upset that she hates me now, but I know I did the*

*right thing. Hopefully when she gets out of treat-*
*ment she'll see that I just wanted to help.*
—Catherine

## HOW TO BE SUPPORTIVE DURING RECOVERY

Once a friend has been identified with an eating dis-order, she should begin treatment. Recovery is a long, painful process with many ups and downs. During this time, it is essential that she be sur-rounded by supportive people. There are many things you can do to show her that you care and that you believe she can recover.

The main thing is not to nag her about her weight or food. She should have a therapist and nutritionist working with her on those issues. Your role is to let her know that she is a great person no matter what she eats or how much she weighs.

But be careful about what you say and how you phrase things. Her self-esteem is very fragile right now and any comments about her appearance will likely be misconstrued. Statements like, "You're looking really good now" could make her think she is getting fat. Try to take the focus off her appear-ance and place it on her character and abilities instead. To do this, it may help to get her involved in new activities. Part of having an eating disorder is closing yourself off to the rest of the world. By get-ting her involved with others, you'll help her see beyond the disordered mind-set.

Try not to give advice or be too judgmental. If she asks your opinion, don't try to be a therapist. Simply say what you see without analyzing it. Stress how much you care for her and that you are worried about her health. Let her know that you are there to support her whenever she needs it. Be a good listener and don't always interject with your own thoughts and feelings.

Finally, understand that you cannot fix the problem. Eating disorders are complex coping mechanisms developed to deal with painful issues. It is often difficult even for trained professionals to get at the root of the problem. You should not expect yourself to be able to help in those areas. Ultimately recovery is up to the person with the disorder. All you can do is provide all the love and support your friend needs to get through the hard times.

## THINGS TO KEEP IN MIND IF YOU HAVE A FRIEND GOING THROUGH TREATMENT:

- ⊙ Remember that eating disorders are not about food and that there are no simple solutions.

- ⊙ Be patient and supportive.

- ⊙ Explore your own views on food, weight, and body image.

- ⊙ Do not make any comments about appearance.

- ⊙ Do not speak in judgmental terms.

- ⊙ Don't engage in struggles over food.

- ⊙ Recognize your own limits.

# Glossary

**amenorrhea**   The loss of the menstrual cycle in females.

**anemia**   A medical condition resulting from a low red blood cell count.

**anorexia nervosa**   A type of eating disorder characterized by self-imposed starvation.

**atrophy**   When muscles decrease in size.

**binge eating disorder (BED)**   An eating disorder characterized by consuming excessive amounts of food without purging to remove it from the body.

**bingeing**   Eating large quantities of food during a specific time period.

**bulimia nervosa**   An eating disorder characterized by excessive bingeing followed by purging.

**calorie**   A unit of measurement that indicates how much energy is produced in the human body by food.

**cognitive behavioral therapy**   A type of therapy that focuses on changing to healthier ways of thinking and behaving.

**compulsive exercise disorder**   A type of eating disorder in which calories are purged from the system through excessive amounts of exercise.

**depression**   A mood disorder that causes a person to feel extremely sad and hopeless over a long period of time.

**dietitian** A trained expert on food and nutrition.

**disordered eating** Thoughts and behaviors about food and weight that are not healthy but not severe enough to be called eating disorders.

**diuretic** A drug that causes an increased frequency in urination.

**DSM-IV (*The Diagnostic and Statistical Manual of Mental Disorders, Fourth Edition*)** The manual used by mental health professionals to diagnose various mental illnesses.

**EDNOS (Eating Disorder Not Otherwise Specified)** A category of all eating disorders that are not specifically anorexia or bulimia.

**esophagus** The passage in the human body extending from the stomach to the mouth.

**family therapy** A type of therapy in which family members meet with a trained therapist.

**female athlete triad** A condition found in many female athletes, characterized by disordered eating patterns, amenorrhea, and osteoporosis.

**group therapy** A type of therapy in which a group of people with similar problems discuss issues with the guidance of a trained therapist.

**hypoglycemia** A medical condition caused by low blood sugar levels.

**inpatient treatment** Treatment that is structured so the patient stays in a facility twenty-four hours a day.

**lanugo** A layer of fine, downy hair that covers the body of a person who is starving.

**laxative** A drug that causes a bowel movement.

**muscle dysmorphia** A type of eating disorder characterized by the perceived need to get bigger and gain muscle mass.

**obesity** A condition in which a person weighs over 25 percent more than what is normal for his or her height and frame.

**obsessive-compulsive disorder** A mental disorder in which a person has continuous, abnormal thoughts and feels the need to take a certain action in response to the thoughts.

**osteoporosis** A disease in which the bones lose density, causing them to become very brittle and break easily.

**outpatient treatment** Treatment that is structured so the patient does not live at a facility but receives care regularly.

**physician** A medical doctor.

**psychiatrist** A therapist who is also a medical doctor and can prescribe medication.

**psychoanalytic therapy** A type of therapy that focuses on talking about and understanding under-lying emotional reasons for disordered behavior.

**purging** The process of removing food from the body, usually by vomiting, abuse of laxatives, or overexercising.

**ritual** An action that is repeated consistently in certain situations.

**self-help group** A group of individuals with simi-lar problems that meets without a therapist to discuss issues.

**serotonin** A type of neurotransmitter in the brain that affects mood and appetite.

**therapist** A psychologist who is trained to help patients work out their problems and learn new coping strategies.

**twelve-step program** A type of treatment pro-gram that views eating disorders as an addiction.

# Where to Go for Help

## HOTLINES

The American Dietetic Association
(800) 366-1655
Can provide names and numbers of qualified dietitians in your area.

Bulimia and Self-Help Hotline
(314) 588-1683
Twenty-four-hour crisis line.

Boys Town USA
(800) 448-3000
Twenty-four-hour crisis line for boys and girls.

Eating Disorders Awareness and Prevention (EDAP)
(800) 931-2237

The Eating Disorder Connection
(900) 737-4044
($0.99 per minute)

National Mental Health Association Information
        Center (NMHA)

(800) 969-6642
Provides referrals to local Mental Health Association offices.

1-800-THERAPIST Network
(800) 843-7274
Provides referrals to local therapists.

## ORGANIZATIONS

American Anorexia/Bulimia Association, Inc. (AABA)
165 West 46th Street, Suite 1108
New York, NY 10036
(212) 575-6200
Web site: http://www.aabainc.org

Anorexia Nervosa and Related Eating Disorders (ANRED)
P.O. Box 5102
Eugene, OR 97405
(541) 344-1144
Web site: http://www.anred.com

Eating Disorders Awareness and Prevention (EDAP)
603 Stewart Street, Suite 803
Seattle, WA 98101
(206) 382-3587
Web site: http://www.edap.org

Helping to End Eating Disorders
9620 Church Avenue
Brooklyn, NY 11212
(718) 240-6451
(718) 934-3853
Web site: http://www.eatingdis.com

National Association of Anorexia Nervosa and
        Associated Disorders (ANAD)
P.O. Box 7
Highland Park, IL 60035
Hotline: (847) 831-3438
Web site: http://www.anad.org

National Eating Disorders Organization (NEDO)
6655 South Yale Avenue
Tulsa, OK 74136
(918) 491-5775
Web site: http://www.laureate.com

Overeaters Anonymous (OA)
6075 Zenith ct. N.E.
Rio Rancho, NM 87124
(505) 891-2664
Web site: http://www.overeatersanonymous.org

## WEB SITES

Healthtouch Online
http://www.healthtouch.com

Something Fishy
http://www.something-fishy.org

# For Further Reading

Andersen, Arnold E., ed. *Males with Eating Disorders*. New York: Brunner/Mazel, 1990.

Barnhill, John, and Nadine Taylor. *If You Think You Have an Eating Disorder*. New York: Dell Publishing, 1998.

Bruch, Hilde. *The Golden Cage: The Enigma of Anorexia Nervosa*. Cambridge, MA: Harvard University Press, 1978.

Chin, Paula. "Emotional Rescue," *People*, November 8, 1999, pp. 128–137.

Claude-Pierre, Peggy. *The Secret Language of Eating Disorders*. New York: Times Books, 1997.

Costin, Carolyn. *The Eating Disorder Sourcebook*. Los Angeles, CA: Lowell House, 1997.

Epstein, Rachel. *Eating Habits and Disorders*. New York: Chelsea House Publishers, 1990.

Fadia, Vijay. *Eating Disorders*. Torrance, CA: Homestead Schools, 1999.

Folkers, Gladys, and Jeanne Englemann. *Taking Charge of My Mind & Body*. Minneapolis, MN: Free Spirit Publishing, 1997.

Frissell, Susan, and Paula Harney. *Eating Disorders and Weight Control.* New Jersey: Enslow Publishers, 1998.

Hall, Lindsey, and Leigh Cohn. *Bulimia: A Guide to Recovery.* Carlsbad, CA: Gürze Books, 1992.

————, and Monika Ostroff. *Anorexia Nervosa: A Guide to Recovery.* Carlsbad, CA: Gürze Books, 1999.

Hornbacher, Marya. *Wasted: A Memoir of Anorexia and Bulimia.* New York: HarperCollins, 1998.

Immell, Myra H., ed. *Eating Disorders. Contemporary Issues Companion.* San Diego, CA: Greenhaven Press, 1999.

Kaminker, Laura. *Exercise Addiction: When Fitness Becomes an Obsession.* New York: The Rosen Publishing Group, 1998.

Landau, Elaine. *Why Are They Starving Themselves?* New York: Julian Messner, 1983.

Lawrence, Marilyn. *The Anorexic Experience.* London: The Women's Press, Ltd., 1995.

Lemberg, Raymond, ed. *Controlling Eating Disorders with Facts, Advice, and Resources.* Phoenix, AZ: Oryx Press, 1992.

Levenkron, Steven. *Treating and Overcoming Anorexia Nervosa.* New York: Charles Scribner's Sons, 1982.

Maloney, Michael, and Rachel Kranz. *Straight Talk About Eating Disorders.* New York: Facts on File, 1991.

Moe, Barbara. *Coping with Eating Disorders.* New York: The Rosen Publishing Group, 1995.

Moorey, James. *Living with Anorexia and Bulimia.* Manchester, UK: Manchester University Press, 1991.

Pipher, Mary. *Hunger Pains*. Holbrook, MA: Adams Publishing, 1995.

———. *Reviving Ophelia: Saving the Selves of Adolescent Girls*. New York: Ballantine Books, 1995.

Robbins, Paul, R. *Anorexia and Bulimia*. Springfield New Jersey: Enslow Publishers, 1998.

Schindehette, Susan. "Going to Extremes," *People,* October 18, 1999, pp. 110-120.

Silverstein, Alvin, and Virginia B. Silverstein. *So You Think You're Fat?* New York: HarperCollins, 1991.

Simpson, Carolyn. *Coping with Compulsive Eating*. New York: The Rosen Publishing Group, 1997.

Ward, Christie L. *Compulsive Eating: The Struggle to Feed the Hunger Inside*. New York: The Rosen Publishing Group, 1998.

Wooley, Susan, and O. Wayne. "Thinness Mania," *American Health*, October 1986, pp. 68–74.

Zerbe, Kathryn J. *The Body Betrayed: Women, Eating Disorders, and Treatment*. Washington, D.C.: American Psychiatric Press, 1993.

# Index